Rufus Jones (1863–1948)

Claus Bernet

Rufus Jones
(1863 – 1948)

Life and Bibliography
of an American Scholar, Writer,
and Social Activist

With a Foreword by Douglas Gwyn

PETER LANG
Frankfurt am Main · Berlin · Bern · Bruxelles · New York · Oxford · Wien

Bibliographic Information published by the Deutsche Nationalbibliothek
The Deutsche Nationalbibliothek lists this publication in the Deutsche Nationalbibliografie; detailed bibliographic data is available in the internet at <http://www.d-nb.de>.

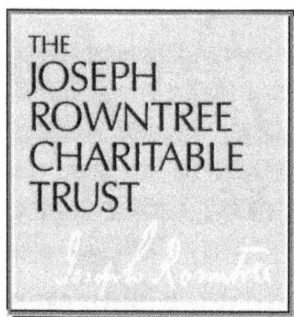

THE
JOSEPH
ROWNTREE
CHARITABLE
TRUST

The publication of this book was supported by
The Joseph Rowntree Charitable Trust, York, UK.

ISBN 978-3-631-58930-4

© Peter Lang GmbH
Internationaler Verlag der Wissenschaften
Frankfurt am Main 2009
All rights reserved.

www.peterlang.de

ش Table of Contents

Foreword

Rufus M. Jones (1863-1948) is undoubtedly the most influential Quaker figure since the seventeenth-century beginnings of the Religious Society of Friends. Claus Bernet's very useful bibliography of Jones' writings reveals the sheer volume and wide range of Jones' scholarship and writings. But Bernet's biographical sketch places all that in the wider context of an amazingly active life. Jones was not only a scholar but a social activist, Quaker minister and organizer, teacher, and mentor. I have been told that his motto was, "There is always time to do one more thing." Clearly, he lived accordingly. It of course helped that two wives, a daughter, and many students were happily pressed into service to his work. Rufus Jones' daughter, Mary Hoxie Jones, still devoted time and energy to her father's legacy well into her nineties.

In the wider Church, Rufus Jones made important contributions to the liberal renewal movement, particularly in America and Britain. Given the liberal emphasis upon the authority of personal experience, Jones' emphasis on mysticism was a much-needed complement to liberal theology and ethics. Through his scholarly work and his popular writing, he was an important influence on liberal Christian leaders such as Harry Emerson Fosdick, Howard Thurman, and Vida Scudder. His emphasis on mysticism in his popular writings was sometimes liberally vague. But his scholarship on medieval mysticism and subsequent spiritualist reformers was pioneering, at least in the English-speaking world. Jones was also concerned for Christian missions. The nephew of Quaker missionaries to Palestine, he was a strong proponent for the updating of Christian missions, particularly through his contributions to the International Missionary Council's *Re-Thinking Missions* in 1933.

Jones' interest in the renewal of Christian mysticism was tinged by the influence of personalist theology, owing particularly to his year of graduate study at Harvard University in 1900-01. *Social Law in the Spiritual World* (1904) is one of Jones' most ambitious popular works, employing the German idealist personalism he had learned from Josiah Royce, George Herbert Palmer, and William Ernest Hocking, together with the new psychology he had gained from William James.

Jones' influence in the Quaker world was extensive. He is the decisive figure in the liberal renewal of Quakerism in the early twentieth century, on either side of the Atlantic. His influence also penetrated well into the pastoral stream of American Friends, although more evangelical Quakers reacted negatively against his modernism. As Bernet comments, Jones' strong emphasis on social reform and progress were intended partly to shake Friends out of sectarian isolation and the mutually hostile camps that had dominated nineteenth-century Quakerism. He was the central figure in the organization and early leadership of the American Friends Service Committee, founded in 1917. AFSC provided much catalyzing influence among Friends and impact around the world. Jones lived to see the AFSC awarded the Nobel Peace Price in 1947. He was less active as a leader but very influential in the beginnings of Pendle Hill, the Quaker study center near Philadelphia, in 1930 and the Friends World Committee for Consultation in 1938. When one combines these with several other initiatives mentioned by Bernet, one realizes that Quakerism as we know it today is largely attributable to Rufus Jones' direct action, wider influence, and continuing legacy.

Critical scholarly reassessment of Jones' work in Quaker history and theology began in the 1950s, with the doctoral dissertation and subsequent publications of Wilmer Cooper. Another important critic of Jones in the 1960s and 1970s was Lewis Benson, who gave more systematic study to the writings of the Quaker founder George Fox. Much of the criticism of Jones' scholarship follows the general pattern of the Neo-Orthodox reaction to the overly optimistic outlook of classically liberal theology, especially after the horrors of two world wars. At the end of his life, Jones himself had already begun to reconsider some of his interpretations of Quakerism. But he was probably the most resilient and infectiously confident leader among Friends since George Fox. His imprint on Quaker faith and practice is nearly as great.

Douglas Gwyn

ش Part One

Biography of Rufus Jones (1863-1948)

I. BIOGRAPHY

Rufus Matthew Jones (25 January 1863 - 16 June 1948)

Rufus Jones was the world's best known Quaker of the 20th century. He made contributions to social work, theology and history, and became involved in peace education before the term was even invented. Leaving behind a rich legacy as a writer, he also stood out as an activist, his greatest achievement being the founding of the American Friends Service Committee (AFSC) in 1917. The ancestors of the Jones family came from Wales and emigrated to America (Hanover, Massachusetts) in 1690. Although Jones believed his family were Quakers at that time, there is no clear evidence of this.

His parents were Edwin Jones and Mary G. Hoxie. They married in 1852 and lived on a large farm in Maine. Rufus Jones was born on January 25th, 1863 in South China, Maine, and was christened Rufus after his father's second oldest brother, who had died in 1862. He was also named Rufus for his maternal grandfather. He had four siblings: Alice Jones (1859-1880), Walter Jones (b. 1853) and Herbert Jones (b. 1867). His childhood and youth were characterized by severe illness, the memory of the preciousness and unpredictability of human existence would accompany him until the end of his life in 1948. A foot injury he suffered as a child developed into a severe infection and spent nine months recovering. Rufus Jones regularly attended Quaker services and Sunday school from the age of ten, usually in Dirigo, which was located several miles from his parents' farm. His aunts Peace Jones and Sybil Jones (1808-1873) and his uncle Eli Jones (1807-1890) profoundly influenced his social attitudes. The three of them travelled throughout America, visiting individual communities which they instructed and encouraged as "travelling friends". Upon their advice, Jones attended a Quaker school in Providence, Rhode Island (Friends' Boarding School, today Moses Brown School) in 1879. Jones's cousin Augustine Jones already worked there, she sponsored him and arranged his admission to the school. In 1882 he attended

Haverford College in Pennsylvania which, alongside Bryn Mawr, Swarthmore and Greensboro was regarded as one of the most prestigious Quaker colleges in America. Influenced and inspired by Thomas Chase (1827-1892) and Pliny Earle Chase (1820-1886), he studied classical philosophy and history there. These fields represented a passion that stayed with him all his life, and in 1885 he completed his studies with a Bachelor of Arts. In subsequent months, Jones taught at the Oakwood Seminary Quaker School in Union Springs, New York (later the Oakwood School in Poughkeepsie). In 1885/86 he earned a Master's Degree from Haverford College. His thesis was entitled "Mysticism and its Exponents." From 1886 to 1887 he studied philosophy and languages in France and Germany (Heidelberg). His professors included Kuno Fischer (1824-1907) among others. At the same time he studied the mystics Meister Eckhart (c. 1260-1328), Johannes Tauler (c. 1300-1361) and particularly Jakob Böhme (1575-1624). Henceforth psychology and philosophy would complement his linguistic and historical studies. Upon his return to the United States, he taught in Providence from 1887 to 1889.

On June 20th 1897, in the Swiss mountain village of Mürren, Jones encountered John Wilhelm Rowntree (1868-1905), an influential English Quaker of a liberal disposition. They would go on to spend several days or weeks together every year until Rowntree's death in 1905. That same year, Jones accepted an invitation by David Scull (1836-1907) to visit England. There he met Rendel Harris (1852-1941) and Henry Hodgkin (1877-1933). They presented joint seminars and lectures at summer schools in England and America on such topics as Quakerism, the Bible and contemporary social issues, such as mass unemployment, the colonial question and the arms race. These meetings led to the creation of one of the most significant centers of Quaker study: Woodbrooke in Birmingham, which would soon be complemented by Pendle Hill near Philadelphia.

In 1900 Jones spent a year at Harvard, where he studied under George Herbert Palmer (1842-1933), Hugo Münsterberg (1863-1916), George Santayana (1863-1952) and Josiah Royce (1855-1916). He attended three courses on the history of philosophy and one on the Old Testament. In 1901 he went to Scarborough (England) to teach at a summer school.

During his stay at the Quaker school in Union Springs, Jones became engaged to a colleague, Sarah (Sallie) Hawkshurst Coutant (b. 1862). The couple married on July 3rd, 1888 in Ardonia, New York. Jones directed the Quaker school at Oak Grove Friends Seminary (Vassalboro, Maine), which was subordinate to the New England Yearly Meeting. His wife taught there as well. Their son, Lowell Coutant Jones (January 23rd, 1892 – July 16th, 1903), whom the couple named after the poet James Russell Lowell (1819-91), was born there. Sarah suffered from bronchitis for many years and had to abandon her teaching activity, working as a housekeeper in Providence, Oak Grove and Haverford, also editing her husband's texts. She died of tuberculosis on January 14th, 1899. Their son Lowell died unexpectedly of diphtheria a few years later. For Jones, this painful family tragedy opened the way to a profound understanding of God's love. Jones remarried on March 11th, 1902. His second wife was Elizabeth (Lily) Bartram Cadbury (August 1st, 1871 – October 26th, 1952). Her parents were Joel and Anna Kaighn Cadbury. She came from an influential and traditional English Quaker family that was renowned for their chocolate factories. Together with her brother, Henry Joel Cadbury, an expert in New Testament studies and Quaker historiography, the team edited and corrected the bulk of proofs for Rufus Jones's 57 books and 550 essays and articles. They also assembled the indexes to many of his works and made it possible for Jones's essays to appear in two and often three journals simultaneously. Mary Hoxie Jones, the only child to issue from this marriage, was born on July 27th, 1904. During this time, the family moved into No. 2 College Circle in Haverford, where Jones lived until his death.

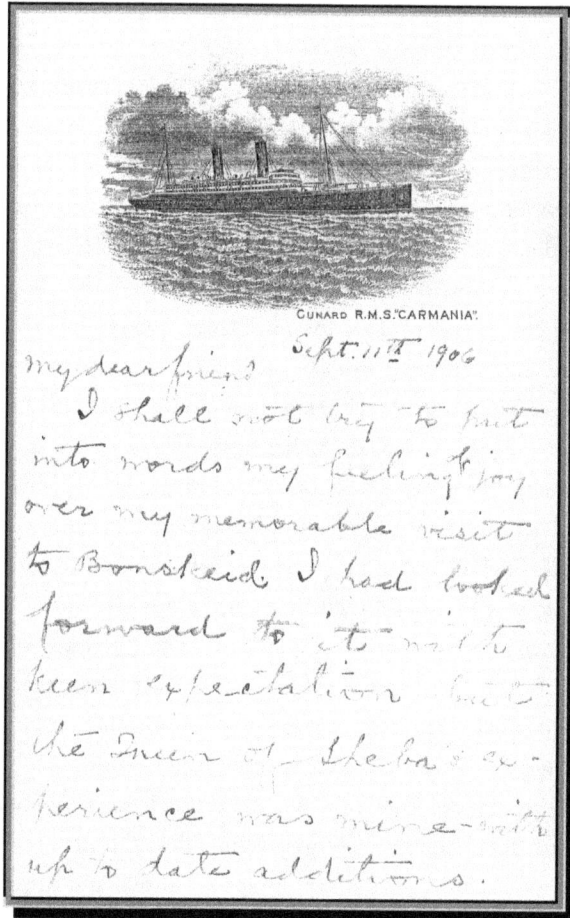

CUNARD R.M.S."CARMANIA".

My dear friend   *Sept. 11ᵗʰ 1906*

Rufus Jones to J. Barbow, written on board the steamer "Carmania" in 1906.

Rufus Jones had already taught philosophy at Haverford in 1893. He had been captain of the student debating club and had been elected the first president of the local YMCA. In 1904 he was appointed professor of philosophy, a position he kept for thirty years. In addition, he served as one of the directors of nearby Bryn Mawr College from October of 1916 until 1936. His teaching activity was interrupted only by sojourns abroad, during which he was usually accompanied by his family. In 1908 he took advantage of his first sabbatical (an opportunity that many American educational institutions grant their teachers every seven years), and the family travelled to England, settling in Charlbury. Jones taught at Oxford and conducted research at the renowned Boldeian Library. That same year, he held the first Swarthmore Lecture on the living Quaker faith. In 1911 he spent several months at Marburg University for academic purposes and worked closely with Pastor Theodor Sippell (1871-1937). The family lived in a twelfth century house below Marburg Castle, an experience that left a lasting impression on Jones.

Drawing mad by Adelaide Newman, Rufus Jones around 1910.

One day before Christmas, 1914, Jones slipped on the ice and suffered a serious injury. A year later, in an attempt to recover his health, he travelled alone to the Bahamas. His ship was caught in a hurricane lasting several days, and he returned to America both physically exhausted and spiritually drained. His dismal condition was compounded by a severe depression and a growing fear of aging. Various health spa treatments provided no relief to his inner turmoil. Not even his many books and his academic duties and honors, which in better days had represented a meaningful life to him, could provide even the smallest measure of comfort. It was all he could do to perform his most basic teaching duties. He began a descent into chronic depression. In July of 1915 his family sent him to Mt. Desert Island, Maine. There he set aside his reading and writing and instead devoted himself to practical and active tasks, such as chopping wood and laying out pathways across the island. Despite the poor weather he laboured tirelessly in nature. He finally succeeded in regaining his courage and confidence. "*Unusual outside weather is only one of our many means of discipline. Much harder is the fight with inside weather and more dreary and pitiless are the fogs and east winds of our human spirits (...). It is not so easy to arm oneself against drizzling moods and drenching tempers within our own interior zones (...). The fight with stubborn inward weather, the battle with the devil in us, if you will, is the best kind of fighting there is to be done, and he who has conquered conditions of inner climate has now the best victories which crown men. Not least is the further discovery - joyous like that of Columbus sighting a new world - that there are inexhaustible resources of divine grace for those who are resolved to rise above the fog and mist, the sleet and snow of dreary inward weather.*" (Present Day Papers, II, 9, 1915, 264)

In 1915 Jones began building a holiday house in his home town of South China, naming it "Pendle Hill" after a site in England where George Fox (1624-1691) had once preached. A short distance from this property he built a modest wooden cabin. It was in this hermitage, undisturbed by telephone calls and visitors, that he wrote many of his texts. He relaxed by working in his garden and playing cricket. He had a sociable nature and was friendly to everyone. Despite his enormous and self-imposed workload, his pace was rarely hectic. He always had time for a brief conversation and was sought out by persons seeking assistance in a wide range of matters. Alongside his private personal activities, he was also concerned with global issues. From 1917 to 1927, and again from 1934 to 1944, he directed the American Friends Service Committee (AFSC), which he also helped to found. This organisation came into being three weeks after America's entry into the war on April 30th, 1917. It oversaw the Quaker feeding effort of approximately a million children in Germany after the First World War. During the war, American conscientious objectors were trained in Haverford and later went on to perform humanitarian assistance in France and Germany. Particularly noteworthy in this regard were the efforts to rebuild war-damaged Verdun. Later on this assistance was extended to Poland (repatriating refugees) and Soviet Russia (famine relief) in close co-operation with Herbert Hoover (1874-1964), the later President of the United States, who had served as Head of the American Relief Administration. The AFSC had not originally been planned as a permanent institution, however. When in 1931 the coal miners of Pennsylvania and West Virginia went on strike and many innocent families suffered the consequences, the AFSC also became active within its home country. Its actions demonstrated the need for a social institution of this kind that could promote and advise many other local initiatives. The AFSC's main fields of activity were such global matters as international understanding, conflict management, political mediation, sustainable development, aid and peace work. In 1947 the AFSC, together with the Friends Service Council (the international British organization), was awarded the Nobel Peace Prize. Jones summarized the AFSC's first years in *A Service of Love in War Time* (1920). This organisation strengthened international aid work, brought a variety of Quaker groups together and made the Quakers known in areas that lay beyond their traditional sphere of activity.

Jones's socio-political activities were motivated by his hope that the Quakers would transcend their previous fragmentation into various more or less self-centred, ineffectual groups and become a movement that would be able to provide significant impulses to American society and beyond. This effort can be traced to the late nineteenth century. Jones first began bringing together the various orthodox Quakers in his home town. He had served as minister of the China Monthly Meeting, the local Quaker assembly, since 1890. This meeting belonged to the regional Vassalboro Quarterly Meeting, which in turn belonged to the New England Yearly Meeting. Together with James Wood (1839-1925), Jones established the Five Years Meeting (today's Friends United Meeting), which began coming together in 1902. It soon clashed with Midwestern meetings that emphasised salaried pastors, revivals, conversion and "programmed" services (services according to a firm liturgy in contrast to silent worship). Jones's mystical understanding of Quakerism did not attract the same support that it did in the "unprogrammed" worship services in and around Philadelphia. In the 1920s and 1930s the Kansas and Oregon Yearly Meetings particularly distanced themselves from the Five Years Meeting. Jones's plans to join the Five Years Meeting with the evangelical churches' "Forward Meeting" became a particular point of contention.

To Jones, the situation of Philadelphia's Quakers since their schism into Orthodox Friends and Hicksites Friends in 1827 was a relic from the past that needed to be overcome. Together with Wilhelm Rowntree, he led the Quakers from the Bible-centred orientation of late Quietism to the modern religious understanding of the twentieth century. His idiosyncratic notion of Quakerism and his liberal theological views were well received, particularly within the Philadelphia Yearly Meeting (Race Street). However, Philadelphia Yearly Meeting (Arch Street) kept its distance. In 1920 the first All Friends Conference met in London and Oxford under Jones's direction. It brought together Quakers of various theological, cultural and ethnic origins from all over the world. On the occasion of this conference he held his second Swarthmore Lecture. Such meetings were exactly what Jones had had in mind. In 1933 he joined with others to create the American Friends Fellowship Council, which after World War II became the Friends World Committee for Consultation. It was designed to co-ordinate and advise on Quaker's international activities.

After his manuscript of *Later Periods of Quakerism* had been submitted to the publisher, finally completing thus the seven-volume history of Quakerism,

Jones relaxed in northern England together with George Newman (1870-1948), William Charles Braithwaite (1862-1922) and Arnold S. Rowntree. In late 1922 he was hit by a car and seriously injured, breaking one arm and several ribs. He hoped that another sabbatical would speed his recovery. In early 1923 he undertook an extended journey to Greece, the Near East and Palestine. That year he also taught once more at Oxford University. In 1926 Jones received an invitation by the YMCA to travel to northern China (Tsinan) to speak on Christian missionary work. In July of 1926 the three-member family arrived in Japan and sailed from Kobe to Tsingtao. In November he travelled on to Ceylon and India. After a visit to Manila he met with Mahatma Gandhi (1869-1948) in Sabarmarti. He spent Christmas at the Quaker school in Ramallah near Jerusalem, and in 1929 he undertook further journeys to England, Greece, Italy and Sicily. In 1932 he spent time in India, China, Korea and Japan in a missionary capacity. He served on the "Laymen's Commission" as a scientific adviser and evaluated various aid projects. His results were recorded in the report *Rethinking Missions*, to which Jones contributed two chapters. Four years later he founded the Wider Quaker Fellowship, an organisation that served to network social, religious and political concerns.

His retirement as director of Bryn Mawr College left him with more time for his international activities. In 1937 the second Friends World Conference was held in Swarthmore under the chairmanship of Rufus Jones. In 1938 he spent two months in South Africa where, as usual, he delivered lectures, worked for the AFSC and visited his close friend Jan Smuts (1870-1950). His return voyage to America took him to Madagascar, Singapore and Shanghai. After the Night of Broken Glass in November of 1938 he travelled to the Gestapo headquarters in Berlin together with George A. Walton and Robert Yarnall to help persecuted Jews leave Germany.

In March of 1947 he suffered a severe heart attack. He died on June 16th, 1948 at home in Haverford, Pennsylvania. He was buried the same day in a Haverford cemetery near the graves of his friends John Wilhelm Rowntree and Isaac Sharpless (1848-1920).

Friends standing outside the Friends Meeting House, East 20th Street, New York, around 1925. The group are (left to right): Henry Richardson, Mrs Mark Thomas, Mrs Benjamin H. Doane, Eleanor W. Tabor, Rufus M. Jones, Sarah Ann Haydock, Benjamin H. Doane, and Mark Thomas.

Jones's theology cannot be summed up into a conventional confession of faith, nor can it be squeezed into a dogmatic corset. He refused any collective confession of faith, either for himself or for the Quaker community as a whole. He thus rejected the "Richmond Declaration of Faith" of 1887, which had attempted to introduce a common creed. One approach to Jones's theological understanding can be found in his mystical notion of religion; in his *Studies in Mystical Religion* (1909), *Spiritual Reformers in the Sixteenth and Seventeenth Centuries* (1914) and again in *New Studies in Mystical Religion* (1927) he engaged in an in-depth investigation into the mystical experience of God within Christianity. In the process he drew heavily on John Wilhelm Rowntree's library, which consisted of mystic classics, esoteric writings and cabalistic texts. Jones defined mysticism or "spiritual religion" as follows: "*A spiritual religion of the full and complete type will, I believe, have inward, mystical depth, it will keep vitalized and*

intensified with its experiences of divine supplies, and of union and unification with an envi-
roning spirit, but it must at the same time soundly supplement its more or less capricious
and subjective, and always fragmentary, mystical insights with the steady and unwavering
testimony of reason, and no less with the immense objective illumination of history." (Spiri-
tual Reformers, 1928, xxix) According to this view, spiritual religion is made up
of mystical experiences, the ideas of the Reformation and humanistic endeav-
our. His essay *Divine Presence in Human Life* (1907) is significant for his special
understanding of mysticism within Quakerism. It lays out an interpretation of
the mystical teaching of the "Inner Light", which he traces to the views of the
early Quakers of the seventeenth century. The "Inner Light" is not something
that has been "added" to human nature but is rather an integral, elemental
component of the human constitution. It is present in every human being,
regardless of his or her religious convictions. The influence of the Silesian
mystic Jakob Böhme is unmistakable. While it is unclear whether Böhme
played a central role in the spiritual life of George Fox, it was Jones who
popularised the famous quotation from Fox's *Journal,* "that of God in every
man," which is today one of the most beloved quotations from the seventeenth century Quaker authors. However, the view most first-generation
Quakers took of Böhme was best formulated by Hilarius Pracher in a letter
dated November 9th, 1676: "Among all the Friends here in London, of which
there are many thousands, I know of none who would embrace Jakob
Böhme's writings and who would prefer them to those of the Friends and
who could thus be called a Böhmist." (*Unschuldige Nachrichten,* VIII, Leipzig
1706, pp. 432-446, here 436/7). Alongside Böhme, Jones also concerned himself with Valentin Weigel (1533-1588), Hans Denck (1495-1527), Johann
Bünderlin (died 1533), Christian Entfelder, Sebastian Franck (1499-1543) and
Caspar Schwenckfeld (1489-1561). These men were all grouped together in
the category of the "left wing of the Reformation" (in *Spiritual Reformers,*
1914), a term that Roland Bainton (1894-1984) would later popularise. Jones
himself displayed distaste for the "left wing" of Quaker history. His attempt
to classify James Nayler (c. 1617-1660) and his circle to the Ranters, a radical
splinter group with enthusiastic traits, is not particularly convincing. Many

things that failed to satisfy Jones's need for order and taxonomy quickly attracted his disapproval.

Like few scholars before him, Rufus Jones succeeded in phrasing his mystic vision in a form intelligible to all and presenting it to a wide audience. He frequently preached for up to forty-five minutes – often several times a week – in Quaker meetings, in churches of various denominations and at universities. In Haverford he regularly attended the "Fifth Day Meeting", which took place on the college campus. His addresses were well regarded and were in high demand at weddings, funerals and family celebrations. He always spoke freely without prepared notes. He knew the Bible like few Quakers of his time and often related the experiences and insights of the Old Testament prophets to the moral, political and cultural conditions of the twentieth century. As an author, Rufus Jones was active in many fields at the same time and on a high level. Aside from Quaker history, his work on the Church Fathers, such as his compilation of writings by Clemens of Alexandria (150-215), published in 1914, is noteworthy, as is his best known work of church history, *The Church's Debt to Heretics* (1924). His *Social Law in the Spiritual World* (1904) was largely influenced by modern psychology, which Jones observed with great interest from America. The focal point of his publications lay in Quaker history, which he studied and taught throughout his life. His *Quakers in the American Colonies* (1911) and *The Later Periods of Quakerism* (2 vols., 1921) became standard texts. These volumes appeared within a series that Jones had developed in tandem with Rowntree. The seven-volume work, with considerable input from William Charles Braithwaite, was not completed until 1921. The individual volumes are entitled: *Studies in Mystical Religion* (1909), *Spiritual Reformers in the Sixteenth and Seventeenth Centuries, The Beginnings of Quakerism* (William Charles Braithwaite, 1919), *Second Period of Quakerism* (William Charles Braithwaite, 1919), *Quakers in the American Colonies* (1911) and *Later Periods of Quakerism* (1921).

Alongside his scholarly and pastoral activities, Jones felt a powerful urge to proclaim his inner experiences to the public. His first autobiography, *Finding the Trail of Life*, appeared as early as 1926. A revised version, *A Small-*

Town Boy, was published in 1941. Additional autobiographical books include *The Trail of Life in College* (1929) und *The Trail of Life in the Middle Years* (1934). While Mary Hoxie Jones's biography includes further important and otherwise unavailable information, her evaluation of her husband is characterised by an understandable yet uncritical point of view. Rufus is thereby stylised as a prophet and hero. We learn, for example, that his future genius already displayed itself during his childhood and youth in the form of signs and prophecies. Finally, his children's books are worthy of mention: a collection of Old Testament biographies appeared under the title *Hebrew Heroes* (1911) and was published in several editions.

Alongside his monographs, Jones had been extremely active as an editor. He gained his first experience as editor of *The Haverfordian*. From 1893 to 1894 he was the sole editor of the journal *The Friends Review*. Under his urging, *The Friends Review* and *The Christian Worker*, which was published as a western version of *The Friends Review*, was united to create *The American Friend*. He presided over this journal from its founding until October 1912. In 1909 he also began publishing the *Religion of Life Series*, and he edited *The Homiletic Review* from 1917 to 1920. Starting in 1938 he edited the *Great Issues of Life Series*, and in 1913 he developed the idea of founding an American-British Quaker journal. From January 1914 to December 1915 he was the editor of *The Present Day Papers, A Monthly Journal for the Presentation of Vital and Spiritual Christianity*. The First World War brought further issues of this international journal to a halt. As the editor of these various journals he wrote numerous columns and editorials which usually appeared without his name. While these articles should be included among his works, such short works have largely been left out of the bibliography (see below), particularly when they cannot be clearly identified through initials. Nor have his contributions to daily newspapers, such as the Bombay Chronicle, been included.

Post card in Germany, distributed in Germany around 1925.

With his publications, Jones influenced an entire generation of Quaker scholars, also through his teaching activity and his supervision of scholarly studies. The important studies suggested, promoted and influenced by him include M. Hist's book on the peace testimony, E.B. Emmot's history of the Quakers in the seventeenth century and Henry Cadbury's edition of *The Book of Miracles* by George Fox. He personally promoted and sponsored Douglas Steere (1901-95) and Thomas Kelly (1893-1941), who taught philosophy and religion in Haverford. Jones encouraged Howard Brinton (1884-1973) to join with his wife Anna Brinton and develop the Pendle Hill Quaker centre near Philadelphia, which they then went on to operate for many years. All of these personalities shared Jones's mystical view of Quakerism and proclaimed a liberal theology which became increasingly concentrated along the East Coast, particularly in the Philadelphia Yearly Meeting. Jones delivered an annual speech on current issues at Harvard university, gaining considerable influence on the country's elite far beyond the bounds of the Quaker community. He received numerous honorary doctorates, for example a Litt. D. (Doctor of Letters) from William Penn College in 1898, a D.D. (Doctor of Divinity) from Harvard in 1920 and an LLD. (Doctor of Law) from Haverford College in 1922. Over the course of his life he received a total of twelve such honorary degrees. He also regularly spoke at Yale, Columbia, Vanderbilt, Stanford, at the University of Southern California and also at the theology departments of Oberlin and Rochester. He delivered numerous speeches during his seventeen visits to England. Since 1953 he has been honored in the United States by a "Rufus Jones Lecture", which is delivered at the annual Friends General Conference.

ش Part Two

Selected Writings of Rufus Jones

II. SELECTED WRITINGS

A postponed heaven

From: Practical Christianity (Philadelphia 1899), pp.54-56.

It is not easy to talk or write on the "doctrine" or "experience" of holiness so that anybody else shall be satisfied with what we say. In fact it is very much like trying to give a good definition of "Love," or of "Life." When we approach these supreme subjects the best we can do is to stammer out our meaning, and we either say too little or too much.

There surely has been a good deal of unwise teaching on this subject, as there has on almost every phase of spiritual experience, but that ought not to blind our eyes to the real fact – the mighty truth - that Jesus Christ expects *us* to be complete in Him, and that the burden of His prayer, - which Christians of all ages have used, - is that God's will may be done in earth even as it is in heaven.

It is certainly true that the Christian standard has been kept too low rather than too high. Most Christians apparently never imagine that they are expected to be "perfect." They quote the old proverbs glibly: "To err is human," "man is as prone to err as the sparks to fly upward," and they conclude that the line of life is bound to be a wavy one, full of bends and curves - never straight onward. They believe that this world is a vale of sin; it is no place for white robes and palm branches, and triumphant songs. These will come only when we get to the heaven beyond the stars, and temptations no more assail us. Heaven is always postponed; it is a place always hoped for, never realized.

It is our personal opinion that this "easy creed," this low standard, this postponement of heavenly joys, is just the reason why the church has no more spiritual power in this present world. He who expects little, gets little; he who thinks that Christian life is bound to be streaked with black and white like a checker board, will of course never rise beyond that kind of life, and he who never realizes that Christ's purpose is to make a "new creature," can only testify that "the kingdom of heaven is at hand," he can never say, "the kingdom of heaven has come!"

There are dangers of course when mortal, human beings go around declaring themselves to be "above sin," "free from law," and "perfect," but all this comes from misunderstanding what holiness is. Holiness is perfect love of God's will, and a perfect determination to live in His will. It does not take the Christian out of this world, it does not make him infallible, it does not relieve him of temptation, it does not make him a law unto himself, it does not allow him to boast of his sinlessness or his spiritual power.

It is simply a condition of heart into which Christ brings His disciples, where sin is hated and God's will is chosen, so far as it is known, above everything else. Love becomes the law of life, and the soul realizes that heaven is not a remote place, but a present fact. The kingdom of heaven has come wherever the King holds sway. This is no impossible doctrine, it is no experience reserved for a few rare saints. It is the privilege and should be the attainment of us all.

Diversions and recreations

From: Practical Christianity (Philadelphia 1899), pp.77-79.

Was there ever a Christian outside the monastery, who did not have to ask at some time in his life, "What kind of diversion is consistent with my Christian profession?" Was there ever a Christian parent who did not find it hard to know just where to draw the line of permissions and prohibitions for the unformed boy or girl?

Every growing person, perhaps every person, needs some recreation, some relaxation from the strain of work, some diversion from strenuous life. It is a necessity to good, healthy, genuine living, and without it the sap of life dries up and the man becomes like a machine. Alternation is woven everywhere in the Divine plan for the universe. Ebb and flow, day and night, summer and winter, joy and sorrow, toil and refreshment are involved in the structure of things.

Take away the recreation and the periods of unbending and you cut the nerve of genuine effort and shrivel the muscles of toil. But on the other hand almost every form of recreation and diversion is open to abuse, and some forms lead to positive immorality. We must have the world to live in, and we have to use it for our needs; but we find at once that it often soils where we touch it, and that too often, when we go to it for recreation, it takes advantage of us and unmakes rather than recreates us. So that it becomes a difficult problem to find proper diversion without at the same time carrying away upon us the dark touch-spots of the world. Every game can be gambled with, every harmless pastime may be pushed to a dangerous extreme, and joyous play may lead to an unsuspected sin. There is nothing on earth that is not open to excess, and the pleasure-seeker is always walking a path beset with pitfalls and intersected at every point with bye-paths, which lead gradually into real sins.

It may do some good to mark out a few forms of recreation as peculiarly bad and dangerous, and to warn all Christians away from them, and there are certain diversions and amusements which must be prohibited to the young while they are undeveloped and immature. But the only real remedy for this difficulty which we are discussing is the development of a strong spiritual life and a genuine moral character. A person will eventually sag down and drift into a low and harmful form of diversion if he has not cultivated a taste for something higher and purer. You cannot keep people out of sin in this world by preaching sensational sermons against certain forms of evil, while sometimes the very description of the evil kindles a desire to try it. The only way to keep a boy out of the lurking traps of sin is to get him in love with something holy, and get his soul set upon a high aim and a true life. He must be made to feel that there is no pleasure or recreation in anything that makes him less manly, and pure, or that interferes at all in his purpose for life. The

best way to steer a young person through the dangers attending recreation is
to help him see the positive side of life, and go to work to help him put on
the whole armor of God, that he may withstand in the evil day. The formation of spiritual character - putting on Christ literally - is the only sure way to
be ready to meet the open doors to forbidden pleasures, and this is the first
business of every Christian parent and of every Christian church.

Not cunningly devised fables

From: Practical Christianity (Philadelphia 1899), pp.127-129.

We have no difficulty in putting our faith in things which we know are real,
and the moment we establish the reality of any fact, it at once affects our actions accordingly. Nobody starts for the Klondike until he has evidence which
convinces him that the coveted yellow dust is really there. But as soon as the
reality is established the gold seeker forgets every obstacle and acts upon his
belief. People laughed at the theory of Columbus until he gave convincing
evidence of its reality, and then ship after ship was pointed toward the west
and the new world became as definite a country as the old world. The Church
tried to make Galileo take back his statement that the earth moves, but as
soon as the fact was clearly established everybody adopted the idea, and now
a man would be thought insane if he should maintain that the earth had no
motion. So we might go on with illustrations, but it is clear to everybody that
the world believes in a thing as soon as its reality is established, and this belief
immediately affects action.

Now, why are not more people genuinely religious? Why do so few persons seek first the kingdom of God? It is because they are not certain of the
reality of unseen things. The trouble with all half-hearted, compromising
Christians, is that something else is much more real to them than God is.
They look at the things that are seen and they find them real; they look at the
things which are not seen and they are not quite sure whether they are real or

not; and the result is that they seek first the things they are sure of. All who are honest with themselves will agree with us that this is just their difficulty.

Now, the transcendent thing about Christianity is this, that for those who are willing to see, it establishes the reality of God and makes His kingdom one of the surest facts in the world. God is no longer an "unknown God." We are not left blindly to guess about Him and His will and nature. He has dwelt among us. This is the Christian message! The Sun has risen and we have seen its light. The curtain is forever pulled back from before the mercy-seat, and we know the reality of the love of God. It is as much a fact as the orbit of the moon is. The kingdom of God is no longer a dream of poets or a vision of seers. The most matter-of-fact man may see the kingdom of God extending its sway. It is present wherever in the name of Christ a man overcomes sin and becomes holy and righteous. Wherever darkness and evil are driven back, and light and truth conquer, wherever saintly, Christlike lives are made out of weak, tempted, sin-stained human beings; wherever souls are renewed and transformed, there the reality of the King and of the kingdom is established.

The Incarnation of God in Christ, and the unmistakable spread of His kingdom, are two central facts. A person's first business in life should be to grasp their reality. No man can live an easy, compromising life after he has established the reality of these two facts. Let him see the light of the knowledge of the glory of God in the face of Jesus Christ, and let him realize that the grain of mustard seed is really growing into a mighty tree, which is filling the earth, and his whole life will be lifted to a higher plane of living.

The historical and the inward Christ

From: Double Search (Philadelphia 1906), pp.21-53

There was once a widespread fear that exact methods of historical research would deprive us of that luminous divine Figure toward whom the world had reverently turned its face for more than eighteen centuries. Some suspected that our records of His life were crowded with myth and legend, others believed that the singular story which had so profoundly touched the world's heart was the creation of highly wrought enthusiastic disciples. Today, after more than half a century of critical sifting and acute probing, this luminous Life is more firmly established as the central fact of history than ever before.

"That one Face, far from vanish, rather grows or decomposes but to recompose becomes my universe which loves and knows."

It is not my purpose at present to retell the story, or to point out how much criticism has left unshaken. I want rather to show how the historical Christ, as a revelation of God, fits into a cosmic system of evolution and how He is related to the Spirit that witnesses with our spirits and is the inward life of the Saints of all ages and lands.

I shall not use the language or the methods of theology. I shall feel my way along the great arteries of human experience and try to throw light and suggestion rather than to establish some final and complete dogma. To begin at once with the problem before us, how shall we think of Christ? Was He man? Was He God? Was He some miraculous union of two essentially unrelated natures? Here are the questions which have split the Christian world up into camps and which have busied schoolmen in all the centuries.

The difficulty in almost all the theological discussions on the subject has been that they started with God and man isolated, separated, unrelated. No true revelation of such a God ever could be made through a human life, for divinity and humanity on this theory are conceived as two totally diverse natures. Modern psychology and recent studies of social life have made us familiar with a deeper view of human personality and have prepared for a more adequate study of Divine personality than was possible when the historic creeds were formulated. We know that God and man are *conjunct* and that neither can be separated absolutely from the other. There never has been any doubt of man's need of God, but we now know that God also needs us and that our lives are mutually organic. Every clew which leads us to God shows Him to us as a spiritual and social Being - in no sense solitary and self-sufficient. Our own self-consciousness, our own ideals, our passion for the unrealized, imply and involve more than an impersonal energy at the heart of things. There must be a spiritual matrix for this living, throbbing, growing social organism in which personal life is formed. Our own experience carries in itself the implication of a genuinely spiritual Person at the heart of the universe of whom we all partake. The spiritual history of the race has forever settled this elemental fact, at least for all who feel the full significance of life. It is not an assumption, it is not a mere belief - it is involved in all we feel and know and are. But a spiritual, personal Being must reveal Himself. An unmanifested God - unknown and unknowable - is no God at all. He would be abstract and unreal. The least human person who poured his life out into those about him - who loved and suffered for the sake of another - would be a higher being than an infinite God shut up in the closed circle of His own self life. It is a law as old as the morning star that one must lose himself to find himself, must give to get, must go forth bearing precious seed in order to come again with sheaves of harvest. The moment it is settled that there is a divine Person as the ultimate reality of the universe, it is also settled that He will reveal Himself, that He will put His Life into manifold manifestations and that He will find His joy in "working all things up to better," to use Clement's phrase.

So long as the processes of evolution were confined to the plant and brute there could be no revelation of anything but force; or at most there could be only dawnings of anything higher. The forms of life which won in the struggle and survived were manifestations of power - they hardly implied anything more. The tough spine and the strong jaw and the sharp claw were all that mattered. Everything that appeared was pushed into existence by a force from behind. There was no sign or hint of freedom, or of life formed under the sway of a vision or an ideal. Things moved "for a million aeons through the vast, waste dawn" toward a goal, but the goal was never in sight and it played no part in the process.

John Fiske has, somewhere, denied the truth of the proverb that "nature abhors leaps," and he has given a beautiful illustration from the cutting of a cone. If you pass a plane parallel to the base of a cone you cut a circle. If you tilt the plane slightly the curve becomes an ellipse. The ellipse grows more eccentric as the tilting increases and finally without any warning your plane cuts a parabola whose sides curve off into infinity and never touch ends again. Some such mighty leap appears in the process of evolution. Up to a certain point life evolved by forces working *a tergo*.[1] There is a slight tilt in the system and a being appears capable of selecting a goal for himself and of acting to attain it, a being who could live in some degree for a world as it ought to be.[2]

This is what in America we call "the great divide" - the watershed which determines the streams of a continent. As soon as there was a being who could select ideals and live for conscious ends a new kind of evolution began. The other side of "the divide," evolution had been physical, - body, and body function had been the goal. This side "the divide," it was spiritual and social, and the goal was the evolution of the man within man. The things which mattered now were love, sacrifice, service, goodwill rather than "tooth and claw." Before, nature's goal had been along the line of least resistance. Now, the line of March set straight against instinct and along the line of greatest resistance. There could be advance on this side "the divide," only as the ideal became clearer and its sway more coercive.

---

1   The term *a tergo* causation means that what happens is produced entirely by the push or the pull of forces. There is an exact equation - the antecedent *determines* the consequent.
2   It is not true, of course, that there is an absolute "break" in the upward processes of life. Even in the lower forms of life there are hints of higher possibilities. There is an elemental struggle for the life of others which has in it the potentiality of love and sacrifice. But there is no "sign" on the lower levels - before self-consciousness dawned - of any capacity for an ideal, or of *any power to develop by the forecast and vision of the goal.*

Ever since man was man he has transcended the actual and lived by vision, which means, I think, that finite and infinite are not sundered and that we always partake of more than just ourselves. Beyond the edge of what we are there is always dawning a farther possibility – that which we ought to be - the *a fronte* compulsion.[3] This is one of God's ways of revealing Himself. It is a man's chief glory - the glory of the imperfect.

"Growth came when, looking your last on them all you turned your eyes inwardly one fine day and cried with a start - what if we so small be greater and grander the while than they? Are they perfect of lineament, perfect of stature? In both, of such lower types are we precisely because of our wider nature; For time, theirs - ours, for eternity. Today's brief passion limits their range; It seethes with the morrow for us and more they are perfect - how else? They shall never change. We are faulty - why not? We have time in store."[4]

This slow unveiling of the ideal, of the goal, is, I believe, the divine method of making man, and it makes us feel at once how nearer than near God is and how all the way on and up He is in the very tissue and fabric of our lives - no foreign creator who moulded us out of clay and left us to run, or to run down, like a clock.

For centuries man won his slender spiritual victories, cultivated his rugged virtues, sloughed off some marks of ape and tiger and formed habits of altruism under the influence of ideals which the highest personal types of the race revealed. These types of men were focus points, manifesting in some feeble measure the ultimate reality and casting out hints of the line of march. Sometimes they were conscious that they were organs of a larger Life which used them, sometimes they were girded, like Cyrus, for a divine mission, though they knew not Him whom they served. Thus the unbroken revelation of the infinite was slowly made, as the age could bear it - "God spake at sundry times and in divers manners."

---

3   The term *a fronte* compulsion means the compelling power of an ideal which influences by an attraction from in front.
4   Browning's "Old Pictures in Florence".

Strangely enough the loftiest men of the pre-Christian period were always vaguely or dimly forecasting a diviner life than any ordinary type of man revealed. The human heart was always groping for an unveiling of God which would set the race to living on a new level. This longing rose among the Hebrews to a steady passion which burned brighter as the clouds in their national sky grew blacker. There was a Christ ideal centuries before Christ actually came in the flesh, though this ideal was always deeply tinged and colored by the age which gave it birth. But even so, it lighted the sky of the future and gave many a man heart and hope through long periods of dreary pessimism. When lo, a tilting of the plane, and the ellipse becomes a parabola with infinite stretch of curve!

"In fullness of time God sent forth His Son." How shall we think of Jesus that is called the Christ? Speaking first in the terms of evolution, *I* think of Him as the type and goal of the race - the new Adam, the spiritual norm and pattern, the Son of Man who is a revelation of what man at his height and full stature is meant to be; and this is the way Paul thought of Him: "Till *we all* come in the unity of the faith, and of the knowledge of the Son of God, unto a perfect man, unto the measure of the stature of the fullness of Christ." Eph. IV, 13. "Whom he did foreknow, he did predestinate to be conformed to the image of his Son that *He* might be the first born among many brethren." Rom. VIII, 29. "The expectation of the whole creation is waiting for the manifestation of sons of God." Rom. VIII, 19.

The actual fact is that this Life has, profoundly or remotely, touched every personal life in Europe for a thousand years and has been the goal and standard for all aspiring souls. He is the pattern in the mount, the *a fronte* force which has drawn the individual and the race steadily up to their higher destiny. On the spiritual side of "the great divide" the goal is in sight and the goal is an efficient factor in the process of the evolution of the man within man.

But this pattern-aspect of the Christ life is only one aspect, and we must not raise it out of due balance and perspective. *Christ is God humanly revealed.* As soon as we realize that personality is always a revelation of the ultimate reality of the universe there are no metaphysical difficulties in the way of an actual incarnation of God. It is rather what one would expect. There is no other conceivable way in which God could be revealed to man. If He is a personal being; if He is love and tenderness and sympathy, and not mere force, only a Person can show Him. And if we are not kindred in nature, if we have not something in common, in a word if we are not *conjunct*, then it is hard to see how any revelation of Him could be made which would mean anything to us. But if we are *conjunct*, as our own self-consciousness implies, then an incarnation, a complete manifestation in Personality, or as Paul puts it, "in the face of Jesus Christ," is merely the crown and pinnacle of the whole divine process.

If we are wise we shall not bother ourselves too much over the metaphysical puzzles which the schoolmen have formulated. We no longer have the puzzle which was so urgent with them, how two natures, pole-wide apart, could be united in one Person, for we now know that divinity and humanity are not pole-wide apart. There is something human in God and something divine in man and they belong together.

We shall not, again, be over-anxious about the question of nativity. Note the grandeur and the simplicity of Paul's text about it: "God sent forth His Son born of a woman," and there he stops with no attempt to furnish details. John is equally lofty: "The Word became flesh and dwelt among us and we beheld His glory." There is no appeal to curiosity. There is no syllable about the *how*. Two synoptic gospels have given us a simple story of the nativity which has profoundly impressed men in all ages and which will always appeal to the deepest instincts in us. But the *method* of Christ's coming, embodied in these two accounts, must not be forced. The devout soul must be free, as both Paul and John were free, to leave the *how* wrapped in mystery. That He came out of our humanity we shall always believe. That He came down out of the highest divinity we shall equally believe. That He was a babe and increased in wisdom, that He learned as He grew, that He was tempted and learned through temptation, are all necessary steps, for there is no other path to spiritual Personality and He must have been "made perfect through sufferings," or He could not have been the Captain of salvation.

Speculations and dogmas have taken men's thoughts away from verifiable facts. Here was a life which settled forever that the ultimate reality is Love. He brought into focus, or rather He wove into the living tissue of a personal life, the qualities of character which belong to an infinitely good being and with quiet simplicity He said, "If you see me you see the Father."

I have spoken, perhaps, as though the revelation of the human goal, and the unveiling of the divine Character were two different things. Christ does both, but both are one. If you bring a diamond into the light you occasion a double revelation. There is a revelation of the glorious beauty of the jewel. While it lay in the dark you never knew its possibilities. It was easily mistaken for a piece of glass. Now it flashes and burns and reveals itself because it has found the element for which it was meant. But there is also at the same time a revelation of the mystery of light. You discover now new wonders and new glories in light itself. Most objects absorb part of its rays and imperfectly transmit it to the eye. Here is an object which tells you its real nature. Now you see it as it is. So Christ shows us at once man and God. In a definite historic setting and in the limitations of a concrete personal life, Christ has unveiled the divine nature and taught us to say "Father" and He has, in doing that, showed us the goal and type of human life. The Son of God and the Son of Man is one person.

Now comes our second question how shall we think of the inward, the spiritual, the eternal Christ? The first interpreters, notably Paul and John, early in their experience, came to think of Christ as a cosmic Being. They read the universe in the light of His revelation and soon used His name to name the entire manifestation of God: "In Him," says Paul, "all things consist." "All things were made by Him," says John, "and without Him was not anything made that was made. In Him was life and the life was the light of men." John 1, 2, 3. It was through Him that they first learned that God is Spirit, it was through Him that their own spiritual life was heightened and that they became conscious of a Spirit surging into their own souls and they connected

this whole wider manifestation of God with Him. They were right too in doing so. Christ's revelation of God had produced such spiritual effects upon
them that they could now find Him within themselves, for God's spiritual
presence in us is always proportioned to our capacity to have Him there. And
then, too, they were now for the first time able to interpret that which they
felt within themselves. If they found God, it was because they had found
Christ.

But they were right in a deeper sense. If we think of the historical
Christ, as I have tried to set forth, as the manifestation of the Divine and the
human in a single personal Life then wherever man finds God humanly revealed he properly names the revelation with the historic name. The historic
incarnation was no final event. It was the supreme instance of God and man
in a single life - the *type* of continuous Divine-human fellowship. God's human revelation of Himself is not limited to a single date. As Athanasius so
boldly said: He became man that we might become divine. Christ is the
prophesy of *a new humanity* - a humanity penetrated with the life and power of
God and this continued personal manifestation of God through men is Christ
inwardly and spiritually revealed.

It is a primary truth of Christianity that God reaches man directly. No
person is insulated. As ocean floods the inlets, as sunlight environs the plant,
so God enfolds and enwreathes the finite spirit. There is this difference, however, inlet and plant are penetrated whether they will or not. Sea and sunshine
crowd themselves in *a tergo*. Not so with God. He can be received only
through appreciation and conscious appropriation. He comes only through
doors that are *purposely* opened for Him. A man may live as near God as the
bubble is to the ocean and yet not find Him. He may be "closer than breath-
ing, nearer than hands or feet," and still be missed. Historical Christianity is
dry and formal when it lacks the immediate and inward response to our Great
Companion; but our spirits are trained to know Him, to appreciate Him, by
the mediation of historical revelation. A person's spiritual life is always
dwarfed when cut apart from history. Mysticism is empty unless it is enriched
by outward and historical revelation. The supreme education of the soul

comes through an intimate acquaintance with Jesus Christ of history. One who wished to feel the power of beauty would go to some supreme master of color and form who could exhibit them on canvas and not merely lecture about them. One who desired to feel the power of harmony would go, not to the boy with his harmonica, but to the Beethovens or Mozarts of the race who have revealed what an instrument and a human hand can do. So he who wishes to realize and practice the presence of God must inform himself at the source and fount, must come face to face with Him who was the highest human revelation of God. No one of us can interpret his own longings or purposes until he reads them off in the light of some loftier type of personality. That person understands himself best who grows intimate in fellowship with some noble character. And any man who wishes to discover the meaning of the inward voice and to interpret the divine breathings which come to human souls needs to be informed and illuminated by the supreme revelation of the ages.

With perfect fitness, then, we speak of the inward Presence as the spiritual Christ. It is the continuation of the same revelation which was made under the "Syrian blue."

The procession of the Holy Ghost is a continuous revelation and exhibition of Christ within men. Whether we use the expression Holy Spirit or Christ within or spiritual Christ, we mean God *operating upon human spirits and consciously witnessed and appreciated in them.* "The Lord is the Spirit," cries Paul when, with unveiled face, he discovers that he is being transformed into His image from glory to glory. "Joined to the Lord in one Spirit," is another testimony of the same sort.

Unfortunately the doctrine of the Christ within - "the real presence" - has generally been held vaguely, and it has easily run into error and even fanaticism. The most common error has come from the prevalent view that when the Spirit - the inward Christ - comes in, the man goes out. It has been supposed that the finite is suppressed and the infinite supplants it and operates instead of it. This view is not only contrary to Scripture, but also contrary to psychological possibility. What really happens is that the human spirit through its awakened appreciation appropriates into its own life the divine Life which was always near and was always meant for it. The true view has been well put by August Sabatier[5]: "It is not enough to represent the Spirit of God as coming to the help of man's spirit, supplying strength which he lacks, an associate or juxtaposed force, a supernatural auxiliary. Paul's thought has no room for such a moral and psychological dualism, although popular language easily permits it. His thought is quite otherwise profound. There is no simple addition of divine power and human power in the Christian life. The Spirit of God identifies itself with the human me into which it enters and *whose life it becomes*. If we may so speak, it is individualized in the new moral personality which it creates. A sort of metamorphosis, a transubstantiation, if the word may be permitted, takes place in the human being. Having been carnal it has become spiritual. A "new man" arises from the old man by the creative act of the spirit of God. Paul calls Christians properly speaking, "the inspired." They are moved and guided by the Spirit of God. The spirit dwells in them as an immanent virtue, whose fruits are organically developed as those of the flesh. Supernatural gifts become natural, or rather, at this mystical height, the antithesis created by scholastic rationalism becomes meaningless and is obliterated." That is precisely my view and if I had not found it here so well said I should have put the same idea into my own words. There are no known limits to the possible translation of the Spirit of God - the Eternal Christ—into human personality. There are all degrees and varieties of it as there are all degrees and varieties of physical life. One stands looking at a century-old oak tree and he wonders how this marvelous thing ever rose out of the dead earth where its roots are. As a matter of fact it did not. A tree is largely transformed sunlight. There is from first to last an earth element to be sure, but the tree is forever drawing upon the streams of sunlight which flood it and it builds the intangible light energy into leaf and blossom and fibre until there stands the old monarch, actually living on sunshine! But the little daisy at its feet, modest and delicate, is equally consolidated sunshine, though it pushes its face hardly six inches from the soil in which it was born. So one

---

5   Sabatier, "Religions of Authority", p. 307.

spirit differs from another spirit in glory. Some have but feebly drawn upon the Spiritual Light out of which strong lives are builded, others have raised the unveiled face to the supreme Light and have translated it into a life of spiritual beauty and moral fibre. Thus the revelation of God in the flesh goes on from age to age. The Christ-life propagates itself like all life-types - the last Adam proves to be a life-giving spirit. He is the first born among many brethren. The actual re-creation, the genuine identification of self with Christ may go on until a man may even say - "Christ lives in me;" "I bear in my body the marks of the Lord Jesus;" "It has pleased God to reveal His Son in me."

"See if, for every finger of thy hands, there be not found, that day the world
shall end hundreds of souls, each holding by Christ's word, that he will grow incorporate with all, with me as pamphylax, with him as John, groom for each bride! Can a mere man do this? Yet Christ saith, this He lived and died to do. Call Christ, then, the illimitable God." I do.

The meaning of personality

From: Social Law in the Spiritual World (Philadelphia 1904), pp. 49-69

There are many things which we know until we are asked. We get on comfortably with our beliefs until some inquisitive person asks us to state them, or until our first child begins the well-known cataclysm of questions and whys, and we are left never again quite so sure as before. Those of us who teach are familiar with the honest answer, "I know, but I cannot tell", which we refuse to accept, though we inwardly sympathize with the student's difficulty.

We all know well enough what a "person" is until an insistent questioning forces us deeper. But if we are to get to any adequate idea of God, we must have just this deeper view of the meaning of personality, for all our search and research are plainly showing us that the one sure path to the divine Person is through the human person. If the inland dweller would bring his boat to the sea, he must perforce explore the river which sets that way.

We all split the universe into a self and a not-self, and this division seems to work well until we ask where the line of cleavage is to be drawn. We soon discover that there is some of "self" in everything. Is the body the self or the not-self? Is the house I have built, the book I have written, the child who is born to me, *mine* or rather *me?*[6] Everybody knows how a fire, or a financial crisis or the invisible messenger passes and leaves us shrunken because something of our very self has gone. We could hardly lose the stars without losing something of this real selfhood. This means that we cannot sharply cut asunder the self and the not-self. They are not two independent things so that either would be the same if the other were gone. There are no such things as "an inner world" and "an outer world" which are separable. The world which is our "not-me," that is to say, the stubborn outside world, turns out to be thoroughly soaked full of mind. When we say we "know" this world, we mean that *it is a world which can come into our mind, which can be thought.*

---

6   See Chapter X in James' *"Psychology"*, Vol. I.

It is something *related* to the mind that knows it, and if we took out of it all that is subjective, all that our thought supplies, *i. e.,* all of the "me" that is in it, who can tell what would be left!

But for all practical purposes the contrast between a *person* and a *thing* - between a self and a not-self - is clear enough. The fundamental contrast is the possession of *self-consciousness* by the *person* and the absence of it in the *thing.* Nobody ever was a person without knowing it! The "marks" of personality are (1) power to forecast an end or purpose and to direct action toward it, (2) ability to remember past experiences and to make these memories determine present action, and (3) the power of selecting from among the multitude of objects presented to consciousness that which is of *worth* for the individual. But wherever we discover these "marks" we infer that there is self-consciousness, such as we have ourselves. If we found an individual who could forecast, and remember, and direct action and make selections, and who yet did not know that he knew and did not think that he thought, we should decline to call *him* a person. However important these outer marks or "signs" are, the essential characteristic is a unified self-consciousness.

Now do we know what self-consciousness is? Perfectly well - until we are asked. But a *description* of it is never forthcoming. There is nothing simpler by which we could describe it. It itself is ultimate (at least to us), elementary and unanalyzable. It is involved *in* every description we try to give, it is presupposed *in* every effort to grasp it; it must be used *in* every attempt to analyze it. In vain should we try to give any hint of its meaning to a creature which lacked it, and our descriptive phrases are exhausted when we have said, "You yourself know what it is, by having it."

Nobody, then, can be called a "person" unless he bears in the structure of himself these "marks," and still further, unless he knows that he knows. It goes without saying, therefore, that, even though "poets are born and not made," nobody is *born* "a person." Personality is not a primitive possession: it is slowly achieved. No mortal knows, or even attempts to guess, how it can *begin* to be. The difficulty is as great as the difficulty of conceiving the beginning of the universe. Nor can we put our finger on the exact moment *when* a given individual begins to be a person. It is precisely as easy to decide *when* man arrived in the long chain of evolving life, as it is to say when one who "comes from out the boundless deep" begins to be actually "a person." The first thing in the way of consciousness is a dim awareness of organic states - a confused mass of immediate experiences, which not only in babyhood, but to the end of life, make up the core of our sense of selfhood. They give us what has been called the "at home" feeling in the body; but these undifferentiated organic states of themselves would never give us selfhood, or at least it would be a selfhood hardly richer than that of a polyp. Mothers and poets alike have noticed that "babies new to earth and sky" have no consciousness of self. They do not say "I," and they apparently do not discover for some time that they are other than the things they touch. How out of the mass of subjective states, "common sensations," as they are sometimes called, which mark the twilight period of consciousness, does clear self-consciousness arise? It never *would* arise apart from social influence. It would be as impossible to develop a personality without human society as it would be to convey sound in a vacuum, or to maintain life without atmosphere. The child, if we can imagine him living on without a human environment, would never get beyond what has already been called his "organic self," his awareness of certain "warm and intimate" feelings which give him the sense of "at homeness" in the body, and which probably most animals possess in some degree.[7] He becomes truly self-conscious because he is born an organic member in a social whole. Here he learns the contrast between "I" and "thou," "ego" and "alter," and between "self" and "not-self," as we shall see. Almost from the first, as though it were instinctive, the child reacts toward persons differently than toward anything else in his environment. In the second month of life he distinguishes the touch of his mother in the dark, and even earlier than this he has formed a peculiar way of behaving toward persons. But the most decided advance is made through imitation. There are few life-crises to compare in importance with the "budding" of imitation, which is well under way about the end of the

---

7   Could a child grow up with lifeless natures, writes a modern psychologist, "there is nothing to indicate that he would become as self-conscious as is now a fairly educated cat". — Royce, "*Studies of God and Evil*", p. 208.

first half-year. Slowly the facts are compelling us to admit that the range and scope of inheritance have been overemphasized. Much which was thought to be transmitted by heredity, we now know is *gained* by imitation both unconscious and conscious. The child is the most imitative being known to man, and this function of imitation is one of his most effective means for the mastery of the world, but its importance in the formation of selfhood has been frequently overlooked. From the beginning the child imitates *persons.* They are the fascinating objects whose movements fix his attention. The mother's smile makes him smile. The sad face and drooping lip are quickly imitated after the seventh month. The bodily actions which result from imitation give the child an experience which enables him in some degree to grasp the inner meaning of the persons before him. He imitates their deeds and in the process discovers a new and richer mental life, which furnishes material for interpreting farther the actions of other persons. In these responses to personal expressions there is to be found the nucleus of real emotions and no less surely the nucleus of volition. From now on, the child is not passive amid the play of forces in his environment. He learns to act by imitating actions, and through his actions he grows conscious of his powers. Thus through these early imitative processes there arises the first germ of conscious distinction between the *self* and the *other,* and there dawns also that sense of power on one's own act, which is, in fact, one of the main miracles of life.[8] A little later the child begins his slow mastery of human language, through which, as everybody knows, his mental life is unspeakably heightened and his personality defined. Here again imitation is the main function which makes this new achievement possible. The first words are all easy imitative sounds; then when the great secret is caught, progress becomes rapid; but from beginning to end, language is a social creation and could be attained only in society. Without it the gains of the past could never be inherited and without it very slender contributions could be made to the future, and that would mean that without it, conscious life would shrink into exceedingly narrow limits. The selfhood

---

8   See Baldwin's "Mental Development" and Royce's "Studies of Good and Evil", pp. 169–248.

which we know could never be, without this achievement of self-utterance through social relationship. Every step of progress thus far in the path toward personality is made possible by the social environment, and it can be positively asserted that there can be self-consciousness only through social consciousness.

Now as soon as some small degree of self-consciousness is attained the little "person" begins to read himself into the persons about him and through his own experiences they become illuminated for him. They do things as he does, therefore they must *feel* as he does. He quickly learns, however, that in his little circle the persons with whom he deals are very different. He finds that he can act toward a little sister differently than he can toward his father. The nurse, too, calls for a different reaction than his mother. He has a small world of selves to react upon and every experience here enriches his own sense of selfhood and helps him define through social contrasts the "I" and the "thou." Already it is clear enough that the "self" and the "other" are born together, that personal selfhood is organic with the society in which it is formed, but the moment we touch any of the spiritual qualities - even the simplest - which belong to personality it grows clearer still. You cannot sympathize without "another" - another whose inner life you can appreciate and with whom in some real sense you can share. Take away this power of contrasting a self and another with the power of identifying this self and its other, and you have removed all possibility of sympathy. In like manner every possibility of virtue would vanish. But so, too, would the so-called "egoistic tendencies" vanish. Pride and self-esteem and the rest of the list of egoisms go when the contrast of self and other is removed. If I have self-esteem it is because I read myself off as important in the eyes of others. There is no truth at all in any view which makes egoism more primitive or fundamental than altruism. They are born together and neither can claim the birthright, however much one may get the *blessing* over the other. Take away the *other* and there would never be an *ego*.

The point, then, which these facts out of the life of early childhood establish is this: there is no such thing as bare individuality, nor could society be the

result of a "social contract." Individuality does not come first and society next
as a product. Society is fundamental, and it is an essential condition for self-
consciousness and personality. However contradictory it may sound, it is nev-
ertheless a fact that there could be no self without many selves. Self-
consciousness is a possible attainment only in a world where it already exists.
Personality at every stage involves interrelation. An absolutely isolated self is as contradictory as an outside that has no inside. To be a person, then, means to be
a conscious member in a social order. Every effort to discover the meaning of
personality carries us straight over into the problems of the social life.

The world of nature, too, which is the sphere of all our activities and
which we incessantly contrast with the inner self - this seemingly stubborn
outer realm owes its reality and order to this same social relationship. Without
a reliance upon the social consciousness I should have no categories for
thinking an organized natural world. Its existence can never be severed from
that of the social order of which I am a part.

It is because we as persons are interrelated spirits that we have a common world in which we can work out our destinies. We are all inclined to accept "the world beyond us" as though it were given to us just as it is in itself.
We get along comfortably with this view, as our far ancestors did with the
Ptolemaic astronomy, which made the sun go round the earth, until we *reflect.*
It takes very little reflection, however, to disturb us in that easy view. Through
our senses, which appear to be our only means of communicating with a
world outside, we receive nothing but bare sense qualities, such as redness,
loudness, roughness, heaviness, sweetness, pungency, and so following. No
"object" from the world outside ever did, or ever could, come into a mind
through an organ of sense and "present" itself. Perception of objects is an
elaborate process of mental construction out of this "material" which sense
furnishes. Our "baby new to earth and sky" has a "color patch" on his retina
when his mother is in the room. But it is a most difficult and complex process
to translate this flat color patch into an "object," and the mystery is that it
ever gets done. At first when the mother is near, the *patch* is large, and accord-

ingly the mother is *seen large*. When she is distant, the patch is small, and this time she is *seen small*. As she moves her size changes.

No object gets its fixed size until the child has learned how to translate into distance the feeling of the muscle strain which accommodates and converges the eye. Then at length the ether vibrations which come from the mother at any distance are read off as this definite mother of well-known and unchanging size. Of course touch, movements and sound are all the time helping toward this achievement. But to the end of life we have no ultimate proof that objects keep their sizes, except that *we in common with our fellows* act upon the supposition that they are approximately unchanging. And the facts seem to bear us out as we act. Our skill in measuring, which more than anything else confirms our belief in the *stability* of objects, is a social triumph and has had a very slow growth. But we never get to know -really to know - objects until we learn their *use* and their *names*. If we suddenly forgot how to use every object which came to our hand or our eye and at the same time its name refused to rise to thought, we should find ourselves in a world of objects practically unknown to us. But just this power to use and to name is a social attainment. We acquire our skill in "labeling" our objects from our fellows, and without this power our world would largely fall back into chaos. Everything we know about the world, even the most abstract things - such as laws of motion, ether vibrations, atomic weights, multiplication tables - have become known to us because they fulfil social purposes, and because they are verified in the experience of many persons. It need hardly be said that one person alone in a world would have no laws. Succession of phenomena - if we could grant him phenomena - would be the most he could get. He would have no way of distinguishing the reality of dreams, hallucinations, imaginations and real objects. They would all stand for him on the same level of objectivity. A *fact* is a fact for us only because it is there for every sane man. Our description of it tallies with what our fellow says he sees. Our hallucination is an hallucination because we can get no one to confirm it. Our belief in the reality of nature is through and through bound up with our belief in the existence of our fellows and in their testimony. Taste and smell do not give us much sense of external reality mainly because we cannot see or feel anybody else taste or smell things, as we see them touch and see things.[9]

How we come to get an external world at all is a most puzzling question. The easy answer is, of course, something resists us or impinges on us and we infer its reality outside us. We know that we have a mental state, and we infer that it must have been *caused* by something not ourselves. But here we face an overwhelming difficulty. Where did we discover causation—where did we learn that everything is caused? Not *from* facts in the external world, since it is by means of this very principle of causation that we are supposed to infer an external world. If causation is to be used at all as an argument in the construction of a belief in an external world it must be admitted as a primary and elemental fact of consciousness - not as something derived *from* the world. The world as we know it is a world causally organized - a linked and describable system, where everything is related. But it is what it is for us because this process of organization and description has had an immemorial social history. We "find" our world largely because it is already *described*, and we can verify our principle of causation in the experience of contemporaries and the records of all who went before. This trust in the experience of others gives us a common world for social duty, and thus we work out our destinies together. We can act together only after experience has given us some unchanging laws which unify our purposes. We can express ourselves only after we have discovered our common relation to something that will do for a standard between us.

What a world would be out of relation to our common consciousness - a world devoid of laws, a world not causally unified, a world not viewed through our common form of space, a world entirely bare of our "thought elements" - we cannot remotely guess. The world we know is the world which is valid for our common experience. Everything in it is a reality for

---

9   There have been many attempts in fiction to describe the development of a child left on some uninhabited island. One of the most famous of these attempts is in a book called "The History of Hai Eb'n Yockdan, or The Self-Taught Philosopher." It was written in Arabic and was translated into English in 1685. Many of its early readers, including Robert Barclay, the Quaker apologist, took it for a true history! It is a feat of metaphysical imagination. The "self-taught philosopher" and the transmutation of lead to gold are on the same level of possibility.

thought. Everything we know of it turns out to be mental. Even the seemingly stark dead "matter" of which we suppose the world to be made, is matter which is obedient to laws and is soaked with mental qualities and attributes. Is this world which we find in thought the real world, or is there another world out there somewhere beyond, which is non-spiritual but more real - in fact *the real world?* All we can say is that if there is such a world, an independent world beyond, it is for ever unknowable to us. It is as though it were not. From the nature of the case we could not know whether it were or were not. It would be like Alice's "grin without the cat," it would have nothing to express itself through. *Our* world is the one we know. It is the world which rests immovably on the basis of social experience. Examine any object in it and we find our "knowledge" to be rooted in this immemorial social consciousness, through which we have learned to think. Destroy the social fabric and all that we now call "nature" would vanish as the shadow vanishes when the object which cast it is gone. But note well the world of nature is not the product of my consciousness or your consciousness, but of *the total whole of consciousness,* and that proves finally to include God. The world of order and law and beauty is not something which exists apart, something which is *there* before consciousness. It has being and reality only because consciousness has being and reality. The outer and the inner are as much one unity as the convex and concave sides of the sky are one sky. There is no approach to the world at all except through consciousness. We have discovered, however, that our own consciousness is but a fragment. It has its being and reality in a larger whole, without which it could not be. Our two significant conclusions thus far will, then, be: (1) Personality involves a union in a social, spiritual whole; (2) the very basis and ground of the world we know lies in this fact of interrelated personalities. But a deeper analysis shows that this finite social consciousness is a fragment. A later study will discover that the spiritual relationships, the ethical structure of society and the solid reality of the universe itself can be accounted for only on the basis of a Divine Unity in whom all self-conscious persons have their root and life, a living Personality who is what we aim to be. In the old Norse legend the god Thor tried to empty the drinking-horn in the games of Utgard, but he could not drain it, though he tried long and fiercely. Again, he tried to lift a gigantic cat, but could not with all his god-like strength. He failed because the horn which he tried to drink was the endless ocean, and the cat which he would have lifted was the whole created world - the Midgard serpent with tail in mouth, fit symbol of the infinite circle. So, too, when we assay a word about personality we find ourselves in the mesh of the universe. Each self, which seems so easily girded and spanned, is bound into a system of the world, and if we could drop our plummet down through the deeps of one personality we could tell all the meanings of the visible world, all the problems of social life and all the secrets of the eternal Personal Self.

ش Part Three

Primary Sources

III. PRIMARY SOURCES

Education

– Denominational schools, in: Student, 12, 2, 1892, 151.

– Bryn Mawr College. Memorial service, n.p., 1894.

– Around Haverford, in: Haverfordian, 6, 1, 1885, 52-55.

– Progression, in: Haverfordian, 4, 2, 1883, 5-6.

– Haverford physicans, in: Haverfordian, 6, 2, 1885, 72-74.

– Bryn Mawr College, in: Haverfordian, 6, 4, 1885, 102-106.

– The Scholar's attitude and service, Haverford 1896 (Haverford Alumni Association, Abstracts of the Proceedings of the 40th Annual Meeting, 1896).

– The Bible in School and College, in: The American Friend, 6, Supplement, 1899, 43-46.

– Education and service, in: The American Friend, 11, 33, 1904, 540-543.

– Influence of education on religious life, in: The American Friend, 12, 33, 1905, 540-543.

– What is success? In: The American Friend, 15, 10, 1908, 147.

– Quakerism and education, in: The American Friend, 15, 12, 1908, 179-180.

– A mind that found itself, in: The American Friend, 15, 18, 1908, 275.

– The true function of education, in: The American Friend, 15, 33, 1908, 515-516.

– Haverford College and some of it's present-day talks, in: The American Friend, 15, 43, 1908, 679-681.

– The religious mission of Friends Colleges, in: The American Friend, 15, 47, 1908, 743-744.

– The teacher's business, in: Friends' Intelligencer, 65, 35, 1908, 551.

– The educational mission of Friends. An address delivered at the General Meeting of Sidcot School, 1908, Leominster, ca. 1908.

– Address by Professor Rufus M. Jones of Haverford College, Philadelphia 1908.

– The religious mission of Friends' Colleges, in: The Friend. A religious, literary, and miscellaneous journal, 48, 50, 1908, 840.

– Religious education for social service, in: Friends' Intelligencer, 66, 6, 1909, 87.

– Cultivating the group spirit, in: The American Friend, 16, 1, 1909, 3.

– Religious education for social service, in: The American Friend, 16, 3, 1909, 35-36.

– The individual as a fragment, in: The American Friend, 16, 9, 1909, 131.

– Change of administration in Penn College, in: The American Friend, 16, 20, 1909, 307.

– Function and value of the denominational college, in: The American Friend, 16, 32, 1909, 501-504.

– The opening of Pickering College, in: The American Friend, 16, 49, 1909, 775.

– The coming educational conference, in: The American Friend, 17, 14, 1910, 211.

– Evangelisation and edification, in: The American Friend, 17, 35, 1910, 551.

– In quietness and confidence is strength, in: The American Friend, 17, 52, 1910, 823-824.

– One of the things we must learn to do, in: The American Friend, 18, 1, 1911, 3.

– Bryn Mawr College, in: The American Friend, 18, 45, 1911, 711.

– Haverford Summer School, 1912, in: The American Friend, 19, 29, 1912, 451-452.

– To the young man or woman choosing an occupation, in: The American Friend, 19, 33, 1912, 515-516.

– What is success? In: The American Friend, 19, 43, 1912, 679.

– Some educational ideals, in: Present Day Papers. A monthly journal for the presentation of vital and spiritual Christianity, 1, 12, 1914, 344-348.

– Practical idealism, in: Westonian, 21, 10, 1915, 274-279.

– Friends and religious education, in: Friends' Intelligencer, 77, 1, 1920, 3.

– The American parent and child, in: Bookman, 56, 6, 1923, 673-679.

– A plea for American friendliness. Foreign students present unique opportunity, in: The American Friend, 11, 17, 1923, 318-319.

– Some problems of education, in: Westonian, 30, 6, 1924, 122-126.

– The spiritual foundations of character, in: Sunday School Journal, 7, 1925, 423-443.

– Die Grundlage des Charakters, in: Mitteilungen für die Freunde des Quäkertums in Deutschland, 3, 6, 1926, 89-90.

– Study outline, in: Owen, Ralph Albert Dornfeld: Learning religion from famous Americans. A source book, New York 1927, 29.

– Selections (from finding the trail of life), in: Owen, Ralph Albert Dornfeld: Learning religion from famous Americans. A source book, New York 1927, 227-232.

– The need of a spiritual element in education, in: Federal Council Bulletin. A journal of interchurch cooperation, 11, 9, 1928, 7-9.

– Religion in school and college to-day, in: Independent Education, 2, 12, 1928, 5-7.

– The need of a spiritual element in education, in: World Unity, 3, 10, 1928, 16-22.

– The psychology of character, in: The Intercollegian, 45, 5, 1928, 225-226.

– What students need most, in: The Intercollegian, 45, 4, 1928, 189, 191.

– What students need most. They have been told that intelligence cannot live with religious faith, that science and religion are in conflict, in: Epworth Herald, 39, 22, 1928, 378-179, 398; 39, 23, 1928, 2, 3, 22.

– A new science and a new religion, in: Religious Education, 23, 4, 1928, 344-346.

– Religion in school and college to-day, in: Association of Colleges and Secondary Schools of the Middle States and Maryland. Proceedings, 42, 1929, 9-16.

– The trail of life in college, London 1929.

– Religion in school and college today. Reprinted from Independent Education, December, 1928, in: Bryn Mawr Alumnae Bulletin, 9, 7, 1929, 2-6.

– Truth must rest on experience. Dr. Rufus Jones gives optimistic view of
modern ideas. Soul is light of man, in: The College News, 15, 22, 1929, 1-4.
– The need for a spiritual element in modern education. Being the third
George Cadbury Memorial Lecture, delivered at the George Cadbury Hall at
Selly Oak, September 28th, 1919, Selly Oak 1929.
– The new day in education, in: The American Friend, 18, 23, 1930, 451-452.
– The new day in education, in: The Friend. A religious and literary journal,
104, 13, 1930, 147-149.
– The new day in education, in: The Earlhamite. Magazine of the Earlham
College Alumni, 51, 6, 1930, 1-3.
– Have souls gone out of fashion? In: King, William P. (ed.): Behaviorism. A
battle line, Nashville 1930, 344-356.
– Education for human brotherhood, in: World Unity, 7, 3, 1931, 383-395.
– The reality of the spiritual, in: Towner, Milton Carsley (ed.): Religion in
higher education. Containing the principal papers read at the conference of
church workers, Chicago, Illinois, December 31, 1930 - January 2, 1931, and
other contributions to the permanent literature of higher education, Chicago
1931, 3-13.
– Education for human brotherhood, New York 1931.
– Het Heldenleven van Paulus, Uitgevers 1931.
– Haverford College founders' day, October 28, 1931.
– The worth of persons, or, when values become infinite, in: Christian Education, 16, 3, 1933, 177-189.
– Haverford College. A history and an interpretation, New York 1933. London 1933².
– Changing a terminus into a thoroughfare, in: Goucher Alumnae Quarterly,
13, 7, 1935, 6-8.
– Commencement address at Perkiomen School. June 5, in: The Schwenck-
feldian, 33, 7, 1936, 87-89.
– Commencement address at Perkiomen School, in: The Schwenckfeldian, 33,
8, 1936, 103-106.

– "Stand on thy feet and I will speak to thee". The baccalaureate address, in: Radcliffe Quarterly, 24, 8, 1940, 11-13.

– Build anew in your own bosom. The substance of the baccalaureate address given at Earlham College, Sunday, June 9, in: The American Friend, 28, 1940, 255-257.

– "Stand on thy feet and I will speak to thee". Substance of baccalaureate address at Earlham College, Sunday, June 9, 1940, in: Friends' Intelligencer, 97, 25, 1940, 391-392.

– Baccalaureate address at Radcliffe, in: Radcliffe Quarterly, 24, 8, 1940, 11-13.

– Baccalaureate address at Earlham College, in: The Earlhamite. Magazine of the Earlham College Alumni, 61, 7, 1940, 3, 8-9.

– Build anew in your own bosom, in: The Earlhamite. Magazine of the Earlham College Alumni, 61, 7, 1940, 8-9.

– Education for living. Address at the convocation celebrating the fiftieth anniversary of the founding of Pembroke College in Brown University, May 16th, 1942, Providence 1942 (Brown University, Papers, XIX).

Political Writing

– Social law in the spiritual world. Studies in human and divine interrelationship, Philadelphia 1904. London 1905[2]. London 1908[3]. London 1923[4]. London 1923[5].

– Reflections on the election, in: The American Friend, 15, 46, 1908, 727.

– The coming international peace congress in London, in: The Friend. A religious, literary, and miscellaneous journal, 48, 29, 1908, 477.

– The battle with the liquor traffic in the States, in: The Friend. A religious, literary, and miscellaneous journal, 48, 31, 1908, 509-511.

– A new stage in the battle with intoxicants, in: The American Friend, 16, 46, 1909, 727.

– The Philadelphia strike, in: The American Friend, 17, 9, 1910, 131.

– The elections, in: The American Friend, 17, 46, 1910, 727.

– Mistaking the map for the country, in: The American Friend, 18, 18, 1911, 275-276.

– The August character on law, in: The American Friend, 18, 21, 1911, 323.

– The meaning of election, in: The American Friend, 19, 46, 1912, 727.

– The European catastrophe, in: The Friend. A religious, literary, and miscellaneous journal, 54, 38, 1914, 682-683.

– The European catastrophe, in: Present Day Papers. A monthly journal for the presentation of vital and spiritual Christianity, 1, 9, 1914, 247-248.

– "Honor" and war, in: Present Day Papers. A monthly journal for the presentation of vital and spiritual Christianity, 2, 4, 1915, 104-107.

– The presidential campaign in the United States, in: The Friend. A religious, literary, and miscellaneous journal, 56, 35, 1916, 683-684.

– Possibilities, in: The South African Ambassador, 1, 3, 1917, 6.

– A constructive Quaker policy in the present national crisis, in: The Friend. A religious and literary journal, 90, 52, 1917, 615-616.

– A constructive Quaker policy in the present crisis, in: Westonian, 23, 6/7, 1917, 162-166.

– Letter to workers in France, in: Friends' Intelligencer, 75, 6, 1918, 88-89.

– A message to our boys over there, in: The American Friend, 6, 8, 1918, 156.

– The kind of men who should go to France, in: Friends' Intelligencer, 75, 30, 1918, 472.

– English and American Friends in France, in: Friends' Intelligencer, 76, 15, 1919, 225, 228.

– English and American Friends in France, in: The American Friend, 7, 16, 1919, 331.

– English and American Friends in France, in: The Friend. A religious, literary, and miscellaneous journal, 59, 17, 1919, 253-253.

– The democracy we aim at, in: The Homiletic Review. An international magazine of religion, theology, and philosophy, 77, 2, 1919, 89-91.

– The democracy we aim at, in: The Friend. A religious, literary, and miscellaneous journal, 59, 11, 1919, 147-148.

– Our workers in France, in: Friends' Intelligencer, 76, 12, 1919, 178.

– Our workers in France, in: The American Friend, 7, 12, 1919, 245.

– A service of love in war time. American Friends relief work in Europe, 1917-1919, New York 1920.

– Sociala lagar i andens värld. Om det mänskligas och gudomligas förhallande till varandra, Stockholm 1921.

– Why the government relief is not adequate, in: The American Friend, 9, 52, 1921, 1053.

– Some problems before the society. Week-end conference at Jordans, in: The Friend. A religious, literary, and miscellaneous journal, 62, 48, 1922, 835.

– The next President of the United States, in: The Friend. A religious and literary journal, 68, 42, 1928, 921-923.

– Overcoming evil, in: Allen, Devere (ed.): Pacifism in the modern world, Garden City 1929, 39-48.

– El reino de la imponderable, in: La nueva democracia, 13, 1, 1932, 13.

– A new world order, in: The Expositor and the Homiletic Review. An international magazine of religion, theology, and philosophy, 38, 9, 1936, 389-390.

– Rufus Jones tells of visit to Germany. Quaker delegation well received finds friendly atmosphere not wholly vanished, in: The American Friend, 27, 1, 1939, 22.

– The visit to Germany, in: Zions Herald. The independent Methodist weekly, 117, 4, 1939, 88, 94.

– The visit to Germany, in: Friends' Intelligencer, 96, 2, 1939, 19.

– The visit to Germany, in: The Friend. A religious and literary journal, 112, 14, 1939, 256.

– The Quaker visit to Germany, in: Watchman-Examiner, 27, 8, 1939, 200.

– Totalitarism never complete, in: Canadian Friend, 35, 2, 1939, 9-11.

– Visit to Germany, in: Canadian Friend, 35, 2, 1939, 5-6.

– Views on why we should remain away from foreign wars, in: French, Paul Courly (ed.): Common sense neutrality. Mobilizing for peace, New York 1939, 141-142.

– The Quaker experiment, in: What about the conscientious objector? A supplement to the pacifist handbook, Philadelphia 1940, 61-63.

– The American Friends in France, 1917-1919. Together with problems involved in administering relief abroad, by Clarence E. Pickett, New York 1943 (Russell Sage Foundation Publications. Administration of Relief Abroad. A Series of Occasional Papers, 5).

– Our day in the German Gestapo, in: The American Friend, 54, 14, 1947, 265-267.

– Our day in the German Gestapo, n.p., 1947.

– Our day in the German Gestapo, in: Friends' Intelligencer, 104, 31, 1947, 404-406.

– Democracy in China, in: Lee, William Storrs (ed.): Maine. A literary chronicle, New York 1968, 326-335.

Literary Works

– Jones, Rufus Matthew; Birdsall, William Witfred (ed.): Famous authors and the best literature of England and America. With pen pictures and portraits of the authors containing the lives of English and American authors in story form. Their portraits, their homes and their personal traits. How they worked and what they wrote. Together with choice selections from their writings. Embracing the great poets of England and America, famous novelists, distinguished essayists and historians, our humorists, noted journalists and magazine contributors, statesmen in literature, noted women in literature, popular writers for young people, great orators and public lectures. Sumptuously illustrated with original drawings, Philadelphia 1897.

– Jones, Rufus Matthew; Birdsall, William Witfred (ed.): Home school of American literature. Or, easy steps to an education in the lives and writings of our best authors (...), Philadelphia 1897.

– Jones, Rufus Matthew; Birdsall, William Witfred (ed.): Library of the best American literature. Containing the lives of our authors in story form (...), Chicago 1897.

– Jones, Rufus Matthew; Birdsall, William Witfred (ed.): The Literature of America and our favorite authors. Containing the lives of our noted American and favorite English authors (...), Philadelphia 1897.

– Jones, Rufus Matthew; Birdsall, William Witfred (ed.): Shepp's literary world. Containing the lives of our noted American and favorite English authors (...), Philadelphia 1897.

– Jones, Rufus Matthew; Birdsall, William Witfred (ed.): Pleasant hours with American authors, containing the lives of our authors in story form (...), Philadelphia 1898.

– Jones, Rufus Matthew; Birdsall, William Witfred (ed.): Beautiful gems from American writers and the lives and portraits of our favorite authors (...), Chicago 1901.

– Jones, Rufus Matthew; Birdsall, William Witfred (ed.): A century of American literature and the lives and portraits of our favorite authors. Together with choice selections from their writings (...), Philadelphia 1901.

– Jones, Rufus Matthew; Birdsall, William Witfred (ed.): Library of American literature. The lives and portraits of our great authors (...), Philadelphia 1901.

– Whittier's fundamental religious faith, in: The Friends' Quarterly Examiner. A religious, social and miscellaneous review, 278, 4, 1938, 97-118.

– Rufus Jones' selected stories of native Maine humor. Edited by Nixon Orwin Rush, Worcester 1945.

– A poet's faith, London 1948.

– The romance of the Indian heart, in: Maine Writers Research Club (ed.): Maine Indians in history and legends, Portland, ca. 1952, 141-148.

Biography & Obituary

– In memoriam (Pliny E. Chase), in: Friends' Review. A religious, literary, and miscellaneous journal, new series, 40, 28, 1887, 451-452.

– Eli and Sybil Jones. Their life and work, Philadelphia, ca. 1889.

– Robert Browning, in: Student, 10, 2, 1890, 173-176.

– Pliny E. Chase. As a teacher, in: Student, 10, 6, 1890, 313.

– Pliny E. Chase, in: Haverfordian, 25, 12, 1903, 137.

– Fox, George: The Journal. An autobiography. Vol. 2. Edited by Rufus M. Jones, Philadelphia 1903. Philadelphia 1904[2]. Philadelphia 1906[3]. Reprint Philadelphia 1909. Reprint London 1912. Reprint Philadelphia 1919. Reprint London 1924. Reprint New York 1963. Reprint London 1969.

– Whittier the mystic, in: Supplement to "The Friend", 6th December, 1907: John Greenleaf Whittier. Centenary souvenir 1907, Leominster 1907, 2-4.

– David Scull, in: The American Friend, 14, 49, 1907, 779.

– Whittier the mystic, in: The American Friend, 14, 50, 1907, 803-804.

– Two splendid Quaker biographies, in: The American Friend, 15, 9, 1908, 131-132.

– Rebecca W. Cadbury, in: The American Friend, 15, 37, 1908, 583.

– A beautiful life - Ruth S. Murray, in: The American Friend, 15, 45, 1908, 711.

– Memoirs of David Scull, in: Scull, David: Union with God in thought and faith. Reflections on the enlargement of religious life through modern knowledge, Philadelphia 1908, v-xxix.

– Theodore L. Cuyler, in: The American Friend, 16, 10, 1909, 147.

– Anna Mekeel Hussey, in: The American Friend, 16, 16, 1909, 243.

– A century for Whitewater Monthly Meeting, in: The American Friend, 16, 39, 1909, 615.

– Whittier the mystic, in: Whittier, John Greenleaf: Poems for the inner life, Bannisdale 1909, v-vii (Yorkshire 1905 Committee).

– John Greenleaf Whittier, in: The Friend. A religious, literary, and miscellaneous journal, 49, 16, 1909, 244-246.

– The ethical and spiritual message of Thomas Hill Green, in: The Friends' Quarterly Examiner. A religious, social and miscellaneous review, 44, 1, 1910, 33-51.

– Allen Jay, in: The American Friend, 17, 20, 1910, 307-308.

– William James, in: Friends' Intelligencer, 77, 39, 1910, 576-577.

– The death of Hannah Withall Smith, in: The American Friend, 18, 19, 1911, 291-292.

– Albert K. Smiley, in: The American Friend, 19, 50, 1912, 791-792.

– Henri Bergson, in: Present Day Papers. A monthly journal for the presentation of vital and spiritual Christianity, 1, 9, 1914, 270-273.

– Joshua Rowntree, in: Present Day Papers. A monthly journal for the presentation of vital and spiritual Christianity, 2, 3, 1915, 78-79.

– President Wilson's note to Germany, in: Present Day Papers. A monthly journal for the presentation of vital and spiritual Christianity, 2, 6, 1915, 172-173.

– Josiah Royce and his message, in: The Friend. A religious, literary, and miscellaneous journal, 56, 42, 1916, 811-813.

– Dr. Benjamin F. Trueblood, in: The Friend. A religious, literary, and miscellaneous journal, 56, 48, 1916, 927-928.

– Joshua L. Baily, in: The American Friend, 5, 2, 1917, 27-29.

– Joshua L. Baily, in: The Friend. A religious, literary, and miscellaneous journal, 57, 1, 1917, 6-7.

– John Greenleaf Whittier, in: Whittier, John Greenleaf: Poems (selected), Harrogate 1918, 7-12.

– The story of George Fox, New York 1919. Reprint London 1922. New York 1922[2]. Reprint Philadelphia 1943.

– Allen C. Thomas, in: The Quaker. A fortnightly journal devoted to the Religious Society of Friends, 1, 18, 1920, 215-216.

– Thomas C. Allen, in: The Friend. A religious and literary journal, 94, 42, 1921, 497-498.

– Allen C. Thomas, in: The Friend. A religious, literary, and miscellaneous journal, 61, 1, 1921, 1-2.

– George Fox - Prophet and reformer, in: Hibbert Journal. A quarterly review of religion, theology, and philosophy, 23, 10, 1924, 32-42.

– The psychology of George Fox, in: Holborn Review, 56, 1924, 320-331.

– George Fox and the modern world, in: The Friend. A religious, literary, and miscellaneous journal, 64, 28, 1924, 589-591.

– Journal of George Fox and its underlying documents, in: The Friend. A religious and literary journal, 98, 24, 1924, 279-280.

– The life and message of George Fox 1624-1924. A tercentenary address, given at Haverford College, Haverford, Pennsylvania, May 17, 1924, New York 1924.

– George Fox and the modern world, in: Christian Century. A journal of religion, 41, 29, 1924, 916-918.

– George Fox. Bemyndigad översättning fran engelskan av A. Dalquist, Uppsala 1925.

– The psychology of George Fox, in: New appreciations of George Fox. A tercentenary collection of studies, London 1925, 66-85.

– James Wood, in: The American Friend, 13, 53, 1925, 896-897.

– Joseph Rowntree. An appreciation, in: The Friend. A religious and literary journal, 65, 13, 1925, 254.

– Journal and documents of George Fox. Substance of an address given at Arch Street Meeting-house Philadelphia, Pa, in: The American Friend, 13, 10, 1925, 185-186.

– Journal of George Fox and its underlying documents, in: Friends' Intelligencer, 82, 4, 1925, 65-67.

– Friends have sitting with Gandhi. Rufus Jones gives graphic description and impressions of India's great leader, in: The American Friend, 15, 2, 1927, 25-26.

– John Wilhelm Rowntree, a Quaker prophet, London 1928.

– George Fox. Christian literature society for India, Madras 1928 (Bhaktas of the World, 2).

– David G. Alsop, in: The Friend. A religious and literary journal, 102, 4, 1928, 38.

– (Tolstoy), in: Unity. Freedom, fellowship and character in religion, 102, 1, 1928, 18.

– The spiritual life of Baron von Hügel as revealed in his letters, Chester 1928.

– Religion and the family life, in: American Federationist. Official monthly magazine of the American federation of labour and congress of industrial organizations, 35, 10, 1928, 1176-1182.

– The spiritual life of Baron von Hügel as revealed in his letters, in: The Crozer Quarterly, 5, 3 1928, 259-266.

– William H. Taft, in: Bryn Mawr and Haverford Bi-College News, 16, 16, 1930, 1.

– In memory of William H. Taft. Reprinted from College News, March 12, 1930, in: Bryn Mawr Alumnae Bulletin, 10, 4, 1930, 11.

– The life and message of George Fox, Tokyo, ca. 1930 (Series for Thinking Men).

– George Fox. Seeker and Friend, in: The Christian Leader, 33, 22, 1930, 681-682.

– George Fox. Seeker and Friend, New York 1930. London 1930[2] (Creative Lives).

– Thomas J. Battey, in: The Friend. A religious and literary journal, 105, 7, 1931, 76-77.

– George Fox and James Nayler, in: The Friend. A religious and literary journal, 71, 52, 1931, 1183-1185.

– Henry T. Hodgkin, in: The Friend. A religious and literary journal, 106, 40, 1933, 476.

– William T. Elkinton, in: The Friend. A religious and literary journal, 107, 10, 1933, 159.

– A significant anniversary. John Wilhelm Rowntree, died March 9, 1905, in: The Friend. A religious and literary journal, 93, 10, 1935, 199-200.

– Bryn Mawr College (ed.): In Memory of M. Carey Thomas. Addresses delivered at a memorial service held at Goodhart Hall, Bryn Mawr College December nineteenth, 1935, n.p., 1935.

– Mahatma Gandhi and soul force, in: Radhakrishnan, Sarvepalli (ed.): Mahatma Gandhi. Essays and reflections on his life and work. Presented to him on his seventieh (sic!) birthday, October 2nd, 1939, London 1939, 161-166. London 1949[2]. Reprint Bombay 1956, 124-129. Bombay 1957[2]. Bombay 1964[3]. Bombay 1977[4]. Bombay 1985[5]. Bombay 1998[9].

– Augustus Taber Murray, in: The Friend. A religious and literary journal, 113, 19, 1940, 327.

– Alfred Neave Brayshaw, in: The Friend. A religious and literary journal, 113, 19, 1940, 328.

– In memory of Walter C. Woodward, in: The American Friend, 30, 10, 1942, 191.

– President Marian Park's role in the community, in: Bryn Mawr Alumnae Bulletin, Supplement, 22, 7, 1942, 7-8.

– John William Rowntree, Philadelphia 1942.

– William Penn. Apostle of liberty and human rights, in: The American Friend, 32, 21, 1944, 417-419.

– William Penn. Apostle of liberty and human rights, in: Christian Education, 28, 2, 1944, 79-88.

– Mahatma Gandhi, in: Friends' Intelligencer, 101, 44, 1944, 703-704.

– Apostle of liberty and human rights. William Penn, born on Tower Hill, October 14, 1644, in: The Friend. The Quaker weekly journal, 102, 41, 1944, 659-663.

– The radiant life, New York 1944. New York 1944[2]. New York 1945[3]. New York 1946[4].

– John Greenleaf Whittier, in: Whittier, John Greenleafe: Poems of the inner life, London 1947, 7-16.

– Einleitung, in: Tagebuch von George Fox, Bad Pyrmont 1950, 7-12.

Autobiography

– A boy's religion from memory, Philadelphia 1902. London 1903[2]. Philadelphia 1913[3].

– A boy's religion from memory, in: The American Friend, 9, 6, 1902, 124-126.

– A boy's religion from memory, - 2, in: The American Friend, 9, 9, 1902, 197-198.

– A boy's religion from memory, - 3, in: The American Friend, 9, 12, 1902, 272-273.

– A boy's religion from memory, - 4, in: The American Friend, 9, 16, 1902, 367-368.

– A boy's religion from memory, - 5, in: The American Friend, 9, 21, 1902, 461-462.

– A boy's religion from memory, - 6, in: The American Friend, 9, 25, 1902, 525-526.

– A boy's religion from memory, - 7, in: The American Friend, 9, 29, 1902, 589-590.

– A boy's religion from memory, - 8, in: The American Friend, 9, 32, 1902, 637-638.

– A boy's religion from memory, - 9, in: The American Friend, 9, 42, 1902, 806-807.

– A boy's religion from memory, - 10, in: The American Friend, 9, 46, 1902, 882-883.

– A boy's religion from memory, in: Friends' Intelligencer, 59, 37, 1902, 580-581.

– At sea, in: The American Friend, 15, 16, 1908, 243.

– Impression of Oxford, in: The American Friend, 15, 26, 1908, 403-404.

– The experiences of a Journey, in: The American Friend, 15, 35, 1908, 551.

– At Gibraltar, in: The American Friend, 18, 26, 1911, 403.

– In Rome, in: The American Friend, 18, 27, 1911, 419-420.

– In Florence, in: The American Friend, 18, 29, 1911, 451-452.

– In an ancient German city, in: The American Friend, 18, 31, 1911, 483-484.

– In the Wartburg, in: The American Friend, 18, 35, 1911, 551-552.

– In the Alps, in: The American Friend, 18, 36, 1911, 567.

– In Nebraska, in: The American Friend, 19, 24, 1912, 371-372.

– In the great Northwest, in: The American Friend, 19, 37, 1912, 583-584.

– In Bethlehem of Judea, in: The Friend. A religious, literary, and miscellaneous journal, 61, 10, 1921, 145-147.

– By the fords of Jordan, in: The Friend. A religious, literary, and miscellaneous journal, 61, 24, 1921, 390-391.

– By Gennesareth once more, in: The Friend. A religious, literary, and miscellaneous journal, 62, 8, 1922, 135-136.

– In front of Gibraltar, in: The Friend. A religious, literary, and miscellaneous journal, 63, 8, 1923, 133-134.

– Mount Shasta revisted, in: The Friend. A religious and literary journal, 65, 34, 1925, 725-726.

– Mount Shasta revisted, in: The Homiletic Review. An international magazine of religion, theology, and philosophy, 90, 2, 1926, 105-112.

– Letter from China, in: Friends' Intelligencer, 83, 41, 1926, 823.

– In the Middle West of America, in: The Friend. A religious and literary journal, 62, 35, 1927, 787-788.

– The Grand Canyon revisited, in: The Friend. A religious and literary journal, 69, 18, 1929, 369-370.

– Areas of desolation. A letter from China, in: The Friend. A religious and literary journal, 90, 18, 1932, 349-350.

– A visit to the continent, in: The Friend. A religious and literary journal, 108, 8, 1934, 120-121.

– The trail of life in the middle years, New York 1934. London 1934[2].

– Rufus Jones in South Africa. Rufus Jones wrote from Dublin on April 21, in: The Friend. The Quaker weekly journal, 96, 19, 1938, 400-401.

– Experiences in South Africa, in: The American Friend, 26, 6, 1938, 130.

– Letters from Rufus Jones, in: Friends' Intelligencer, 95, 95, 1938, 349-350.

– American Friends in wartime, in: The Friend. The Quaker weekly journal, 97, 41, 1939, 825.

– A small-town boy, New York 1941. Toronto 1941[2].

– A Quaker boy goes to meeting, in: Wagenknecht, Edward (ed.): When I was a child. An anthology, New York 1946, 289-299.

– The luminous trail, New York 1947. New York 1949[2].

– My visit to Mahatma Gandhi, in: Shukla, Chandrashanker (ed.): Incidents of Gandhiji's life. By fifty-four contributors, Bombay 1949, 93-94.

– Addresses about South China, South China 1955.

Mysticism

– The Mystics, in: The Friend. A religious, literary, and miscellaneous journal, 40, 33, 1900, 535-536.

– The mysticism of St. John, 1, in: Present Day Papers, 5, 45, 1902, 62-71.

– The mysticism of St. John, 2, in: Present Day Papers, 5, 46, 1902, 95-104.

– Essays. Studies in New Testament mysticism, London 1902.

– Studies in mystical religion, London 1909. Reprint London 1919. Reprint London 1923. Reprint London 1936 (The Quaker History Series, 1). Reprint New York 1944. Reprint New York 1970.

– Mystical religion, in: The Friend. A religious, literary, and miscellaneous journal, 49, 19, 1909, 291-293.

– Mystery, in: The American Friend, 19, 31, 1912, 481-484.

– The rural problem, in: The American Friend, 29, 32, 1912, 499-500.

– The mystery of goodness, in: Present Day Papers. A monthly journal for the presentation of vital and spiritual Christianity, 1, 10, 1914, 277-279.

– Mysticism and Quakerism, in: The Friend. A religious, literary, and miscellaneous journal, 53, 40, 1913, 635-637.

– Mysticism in present day religion, n.p., 1915.

– Mysticism in present-day religion, in: The Harvard Theological Review, 8, 2, 1915, 155-165.

– Special reading list: mysticism, Boston 1916.

– Standing for a spiritual world, in: The Friend. A religious, literary, and miscellaneous journal, 56, 13, 1916, 193-195.

– Mysticism. A selected bibliography, in: Boston General Theological Library Bulletin, 9, 10, 1916, 11-15.

– Prayer and the mystic vision, in: Anson, Harold; Bevan, Edwyn (ed.): Concerning prayer. Its nature, its difficulties and its value, London 1916, 105-132.

– The devotional hour. 1. The central act of religion, in: The Homiletic Review. An international magazine of religion, theology, and philosophy, 73, 3, 1917, 175-176.

– The devotional hour. 2. The miracle again, in: The Homiletic Review. An international magazine of religion, theology, and philosophy, 73, 4, 1917, 261-262.

– The devotional hour. 3. Behold, in: The Homiletic Review. An international magazine of religion, theology, and philosophy, 73, 5, 1917, 347-348.

– The devotional hour. 4. Faith as a way of life, in: The Homiletic Review. An international magazine of religion, theology, and philosophy, 73, 6, 1917, 433-434.

– The devotional hour. 5. The fact of "must", in: The Homiletic Review. An international magazine of religion, theology, and philosophy, 74, 1, 1917, 3-4.

– The devotional hour. 6. Where love breaks through, in: The Homiletic Review. An international magazine of religion, theology, and philosophy, 74, 2, 1917, 89-90.

– The devotional hour. 7. Truth in the inward parts, in: The Homiletic Review. An international magazine of religion, theology, and philosophy, 74, 3, 1917, 175-176.

– The devotional hour. 8. The all for the all, in: The Homiletic Review. An international magazine of religion, theology, and philosophy, 74, 4, 1917, 261-262.

– The devotional hour. 9. Consecration, in: The Homiletic Review. An international magazine of religion, theology, and philosophy, 74, 5, 1917, 347-348.

– The devotional hour. 10. The Gospel of God with us, in: The Homiletic Review. An international magazine of religion, theology, and philosophy, 74, 6, 1917, 433-434.

– The miracle again, in: The Friend. A religious, literary, and miscellaneous journal, 57, 13, 1917, 229-230.

– Spiritual interpretation of life, in: The American Friend, 5, 49, 1917, 968-971.

– The world within, New York 1918. Reprint New York 1921. Reprint New York 1930.

– The inner issue in Gethsemane, in: The Friend. A religious, literary, and miscellaneous journal, 58, 24, 1918, 381-382.

– The spirit of the beatitudes, in: Friends' Intelligencer, 75, 42, 1918, 659-660.

– The devotional hour. The new born out of the old, in: The Homiletic Review. An international magazine of religion, theology, and philosophy, 77, 1, 1919, 3-5.

– Psychology and the spiritual life, in: Journal of Religion, 1, 5, 1921, 449-461.

– Mystic's experience of God, in: The Atlantic Monthly, 128, 11, 1921, 637-645.

– The mysticism of Meister Eckhart, in: Sneath, Elias Hershey (ed.): At one with the invisible. Studies in mysticism, New York 1921, 199-212.

– The mysticism of George Fox, in: Sneath, Elias Hershey (ed.): At one with the invisible. Studies in mysticism. New York 1921, 240-259.

– Spiritual energies in daily life. New York 1922. New York 1924[2]. New York 1928[3]. Reprint New York 1936. New York 1949[2]. Reprint Philadelphia 1961.

– The world within the world, in: Christian Century. A journal of religion, 29, 18, 1922, 558-560.

– Helps toward an efficient spiritual life, in: The Friend. A religious, literary, and miscellaneous journal, 1923, 63, 46, 898-899.

– Death as a spiritual fact, in: The Friend. A religious, literary, and miscellaneous journal, 63, 15, 1923, 261-262.

– Mysticism in Robert Browning, in: Biblical Review, 8, 2, 1923, 229-245.

– Fundamental ends of life, New York 1924. London 1924[2]. New York
1925[3]. New York 1930[3].

– Practical mystics, in: The Friend. A religious and literary journal, 65, 28,
1925, 611-612.

– Mysticism and the inner life, in: Peake, A. S. (ed.): Christianity and modern
thought, London 1926, 317-336 (An Outline of Christianity, 4).

– Mystical experience of God, in: Christianity today and tomorrow, New
York 1926, 447-468 (An Outline of Christianity, 5).

– Finding the trail of life, London 1926. New York 1927[2]. New York 1929[3].
New York 1931[4]. New York 1938[5]. New York 1950[6].

– Religious education with the emphasis on mystical experience, in: Reformed
Church Review, 5, 1, 1926, 63-73.

– Is mysticism essentially subjective? In: The Friends' Quarterly Examiner. A
religious, social and miscellaneous review, 61, 10, 1927, 292-303.

– New studies in mystical religion. The Ely Lectures delivered at Union Theological Seminary, New York 1927. London 1927[2]. London 1928[3]. Reprint
London 1936. Reprint New York 1974 (The Quaker History Series, 1).

– Mystik in Amerika, in: Süddeutsche Monatshefte, 26, 10, 1928, 48-50.

– Nature of inspiration, in: The Colgate-Rochester Divinity School Bulletin, 1,
6, 1929, 383-393.

– Vom Sinn und Endzweck des Lebens, Leipzig 1929. Bad Pyrmont 1947[2].
Stolzenau, ca. 1994[3].

– Vom Sinn des Lebens, in: Der Quäker. Monatshefte der deutschen
Freunde, 6, 1/3, 1929, 1-2.

– Some exponents of mystical religion, New York 1930 (New Era Lecture-
ships, 5). London 1930[2].

– God is spirit, in: Strong, Sydney Dix (ed.): How to find God. Fifty best rep-
lies, New York 1931, 37.

– The reality of the spiritual, in: Christian Education, 14, 5, 1931, 603-612.

– Why I enroll with the mystics, in: Ferm, Vergilius Ture Anselm (ed.): Contemporary American theology. Theological autobiographies, New York 1932,
191-215.

– Mysticism and democracy in the English Commonwealth, Cambridge 1932.
New York 1965[2] (William Belden Noble Lectures, 1930/31).

– The eternal in the temporal, in: The Friend. A religious and literary journal,
91, 39, 1933, 829-830.

– The miracle of re-creation, in: The Friend. A religious and literary journal,
107, 20, 1934, 315.

– Parent mystic (Forerunners of Quakerism, 1), in: Friends' Intelligencer, 93,
48, 1936, 801-802.

– Parent mystic, in: The Friend. The Quaker weekly journal, 94, 94, 1936,
1053-1054.

– The mystery of the currents, in: The Friend. The Quaker weekly journal, 96,
13, 1938, 253-254.

– The way of the mystics, in: The Crozer Quarterly, 15, 2, 1938, 115-123.

– The flowering of mysticism. The Friends of God in the fourteenth century,
New York 1939. London 1939[2]. New York 1940[3]. Reprint New York 1971.

– Central idea of spiritual reformers, in: Exile Herald (=Society Schwenkfel-
dian), 17, 1, 1941, 3-8.

– Liberalism in the mystical tradition, in: Roberts, David; Pitney Van Dusen,
Henry; Bennett, John C.; Bewer, Julius A.; Brown, William Adams; Cady,
Lyman van Law; Coffin, Henry Sloane; Hardy, Edward Rochie; Hocking, William Ernest; Horton, Walter Marshall; Jones, Rufus Matthew; Lyman, Mary
Ely; Macintosh, Douglas Clyde; McGiffert, Arthur Cushman; Montague, William Pepperell; Moore, John M. (ed.): Liberal theology. An appraisal. Essays
in honor of Eugene William Lyman, New York 1942, 121-136.

– Prayer and the mystic vision, in: Clear Horizons, 2, 3, 1942, 13-18.

– Mystical experience, in: Atlantic Monthly, 169, 5, 1942, 634-641.

– Evolution of the soul, Lansing 1943.

– New eyes for invisibles, New York 1943. New York 1944[2].

– Jewish mysticism, in: The Harvard Theological Review, 36, 2, 1943, 155-
163.

– Jewish mysticism, Cambridge Mass. 1943.

– The spell of immortality. Being the Ingersoll Lecture on the immortality of man, for the academic year 1942-1943, Harvard University. Delivered in Andover Chapel, April 13, 1943, in: Harvard Divinity School Bulletin, 41, 21, 1944, 5-25.

– Light from the Rhineland. Rufus Jones reminds us of our spiritual forefathers, in: The Friend. The Quaker weekly journal, 103, 1945, 133-136.

– The great mystics speak. The nurture of the devotional life, in: International Journal of Religious Education, 24, 5, 1948, 3.

– Evidences of the influence of quietism on John Woolman, in: Friends' Intelligencer, 105, 10, 1948, 131-132.

– The immanence of God, in: Kepler, Thomas (ed.): The fellowship of the saints. An anthology of Christian devotional literature, New York 1948, 652-659.

– Was ist "geistige Religion"? Bad Pyrmont 1951.

– Was ist "geistige Religion"? In: Der Quäker. Monatsschrift der deutschen Freunde, 24, 8, 1952, 114-120.

– Positive mysticism, in: Barrois, Georges A. (ed.): Pathways of the inner life. An anthology of Christian spirituality, Indianapolis 1956, 240-243.

– The mystic's experience of God, in: Weeks, Edward; Flint, Emily (ed.): Jubilee. One hundred years of the Atlantic, Boston 1957, 363-366.

– The mystic's experience of God, in: Desaulniers, Louis (ed.): 119 years of the Atlantic. Boston, ca. 1977, 289-293.

– Sources of universalism in Quaker thought. Passages from "Spiritual Reformers in the 16th and 17th Centuries" by Rufus Jones. Edited by Winifred Burdick, Cumnor 1984 (QUG Pamphlet, 5).

– Practical mysticism, in: Cell, Edward (ed.): Daily readings from Quaker spirituality, Springfield 1987, 55.

Church History

– Development of professional ministry in the early church, in: The American Friend, 12, 46, 1905, 752-755.

– Development of professional ministry in the early church, in: The British Friend. A religious and literary journal, written from the standpoint of the Society of Friends, 14, 12, 1905, 330-332.

– Development of professional ministry in the early church, 2, in: The British Friend. A religious and literary journal, written from the standpoint of the Society of Friends, 15, 1, 1906, 4-6.

– Ruined abbeys of England, in: The American Friend, 15, 32, 1908, 499-500.

– Anabaptism in England, Oxford 1908.

– The Anabaptists, Oxford 1908.

– A newly discovered early Christian document, in: The American Friend, 16, 13, 1909, 195.

– Caspar Schwenckfeld and the reformation of the "middle way", in: The Schwenckfeldian, 10, 10, 1913, 177-183.

– Luther's visit to Marburg, in: The American Friend, 18, 32, 1911, 499-500.

– Caspar Schwenckfeld and the reformation of the "middle way", in: Hartford Seminary Record, 23, 4, 1913, 96-113.

– Selections from the writings of Clement of Alexandria, London 1914.

– A forgotten hero of the reformation, in: The Constructive Quarterly. A journal of the faith, work and thought of Christendom, 1, 2, 1913, 412-423.

– Quietism, in: The Harvard Theological Review, 10, 1, 1917, 1-51.

– The Anabaptist and minor sects in the reformation, in: The Harvard Theological Review, 11, 3, 1918, 233-246.

– Geistige Reformatoren, in: Mitteilungen für die Freunde des Quäkertums in Deutschland, Berlin 1924, 12, 131-134.

– The church's debt to heretics, New York 1924. London 1925[2].

– Geistige Reformatoren des sechzehnten und siebzehnten Jahrhunderts, Berlin 1925.

– "Seekers" then and now, in: The Friends' Quarterly Examiner. A religious, social and miscellaneous review, 62, 1928, 185-199.

– "Seekers" then and now. The "John Browne Lecture" delivered at New York Meeting on seventh-day, fifth month 26th, in: Friends' Intelligencer, 85, 24, 1928, 465-466.

– What saints and sages see. Two interpretations of saint Francis of Assisi, in: Christian Century. A journal of religion, 47, 7, 1930, 206-209.

– Heretics of the church, in: Expository Times, 46, 1, 1935, 155-160.

– Rethinking religious liberalism, Boston 1935.

– The eternal Gospel, in: Exile Herald, 12, 3, 1935, 11-13.

Religious Writing & Christianity

– The modern Christian's attitude to the Bible, n.p., 1898 (Haverford Library Lecture).

– Practical Christianity, Philadelphia 1899. Philadelphia 1902². Reprint Philadelphia 1905.

– The fatherhood of God, in: The British Friend, 9, 10, 1900, 238-239.

– The fatherhood of God, in: The American Friend, 7, 32, 1900, 755-756.

– A dynamic faith, London 1901. London 1902². London 1906³. London 1908⁴. London 1913⁵.

– Peace as involved in the Christian method, London 1902.

– Opening words, in: Present Day Papers. A monthly journal for the presentation of vital and spiritual Christianity, 1, 1, 1914, 3-6.

– The divine human idea in Paul's teaching, 1, in: Present Day Papers, 5, 43, 1902, 4-13.

– The divine human idea in Paul's teaching, 2, in: Present Day Papers, 5, 44, 1902, 32-40.

– Peace as involved in the Christian method, in: The American Friends' Peace Conference held at Philadelphia, Twelfth Month 12th, 13th, 1901, Philadelphia 1902, 222-226.

– If thou hadst known, in: Friends' Christian Fellowship Union. Monthly circular, January 1903, 5-7.

– Is our religion a getting or a giving? In: Friends' Christian Fellowship Union. Monthly circular, February 1903, 1-3.

– Has Christianity been tried? In: Friends' Christian Fellowship Union. Monthly circular, May 1903, 7-8.

– On the beatitudes, in: The Friend. A religious, literary, and miscellaneous journal, 43, 31, 1903, 509-510.

– Present-day Bible study, in: Friends' Intelligencer, 61, 40, 1904, 625-629.

– The atonement. Reprinted from "The Double Search", London, ca. 1905 (Yorkshire 1905 Committee).

– Development of professional ministry in the early church, in: The British Friend. A religious and literary journal, written from the standpoint of the Society of Friends, 14, 12, 1905, 330-332.

– The double search. Studies in atonement and prayer, Philadelphia 1906. London 1906[2]. Philadelphia 1937[3].

– Divine presence in human life, in: Friend's Fellowship Papers, 1, 2, 1907, 10-25.

– Gains in the churches of the United States in 1906, in: The American Friend, 14, 5, 1907, 68-69.

– The Scriptures, in: The American Friend, 14, 9, 1907, 131-132.

– The Ephesian benediction, in: The American Friend, 14, 12, 1907, 179.

– How shall we think of Christ? In: The American Friend, 14, 13, 1907, 195.

– How shall we think of Christ as saviour? In: The American Friend, 14, 15, 1907, 227-228.

– The church and the temperance question, in: The American Friend, 14, 22, 1907, 339.

– The spirit of fellowship, in: The American Friend, 14, 18, 1907, 275-276.

– A topmost virtue, in: The American Friend, 14, 19, 1907, 291.

– What is spirituality? In: The American Friend, 14, 20, 1907, 307.

– Otherism, in: The American Friend, 14, 21, 1907, 323.

– God's girding, in: The American Friend, 14, 41, 1907, 647-648.

– The glory of his inheritance, in: The American Friend, 14, 52, 1907, 827.

– A first hand religion, in: Baptist Commonwealth, 24, 8, 1908, 6-8.

– When is a person saved? In: The American Friend, 15, 3, 1908, 35.

– The Christian church in the United States in 1907, in: The American Friend, 15, 6, 1908, 83.

– The evangelical note, in: The American Friend, 15, 7, 1908, 99.

– Two types of religion, in: The American Friend, 15, 13, 1908, 195.

– If thou knewest the gift of God, in: The American Friend, 15, 31, 1908, 483.

– One flock, one shepherd, in: The American Friend, 15, 34, 1908, 535.

– The problem of the Jebusites, in: The American Friend, 15, 51, 1908, 807.

– Gains in the Christian churches of America in 1908, in: The American Friend, 16, 4, 1909, 51.

– How Jacob got a new name, in: The American Friend, 16, 14, 1909, 212-213.

– The heart of the Psalms, in: The American Friend, 16, 19, 1909, 291.

– How Joseph got lost and got found, in: The American Friend, 16, 21, 1909, 325-326.

– The virtue-making power of Christianity, in: The American Friend, 16, 22, 1909, 339-340.

– The children of Lamech, in: The American Friend, 16, 29, 1909, 454-455.

– The church and the people, in: The American Friend, 16, 45, 1909, 711.

– "The new religion", in: The American Friend, 16, 48, 1909, 759.

– The outreaching spirit of Christianity, in: The American Friend, 17, 11, 1910, 163-164.

– What makes a church? In: The American Friend, 17, 24, 1910, 371-372.

– The congregational idea, in: The American Friend, 17, 48, 1910, 759-760.

– The spirit of Christmas, in: The American Friend, 17, 51, 1910, 807-808.

– The danger of literalism, in: The American Friend, 18, 5, 1911, 67.

– Treating the Bible as allegory, in: The American Friend, 18, 6, 1911, 83-84.

– A more excellent way of Bible study, in: The American Friend, 18, 7, 1911, 99-100.

– Gains in the American churches for 1910, in: The American Friend, 18, 8, 1911, 115.

– Two types of religion, in: The American Friend, 18, 30, 1911, 467-468.

– How Abraham came to Canaan, in: The American Friend, 18, 30, 1911, 470-471.

– The tragedies of the prophet, in: The American Friend, 18, 41, 1911, 647-648.

– Consecration, in: The American Friend, 18, 51, 1911, 807-808.

– The ministry of new theology and the ministry of old theology, in: The American Friend, 18, 52, 1911, 823-824.

– Stories of Hebrew heroes, London 1911. Shanghai 1920^2. Reprint Shanghai 1924. London 1928^3. London, ca. 1946^4.

– The spirit of Christmas, in: The Friend. A religious, literary, and miscellaneous journal, 51, 1, 1911, 7.

– Worship. The central act of religion, in: The Friend. A religious, literary, and miscellaneous journal, 52, 13, 1912, 192-193.

– Gains in the Christian churches of the United States for 1911, in: The American Friend, 19, 6, 1912, 83.

– The Hebrew prophets, in: The American Friend, 19, 13, 1912, 195-196.

– Religion as appreciation, in: The Friends' Quarterly Examiner. A religious, social and miscellaneous review, 47, 1913, 9-15.

– Christianity in effectual operations, in: The American Friend, 1, 34, 1913, 541-542.

– Is belief in the personality of God necessary for religion? In: Present Day Papers. A monthly journal for the presentation of vital and spiritual Christianity, 1, 1, 1914, 6-10.

– "I come in the little things", in: Present Day Papers. A monthly journal for the presentation of vital and spiritual Christianity, 1, 2, 1914, 35-37.

– In the spirit, in: Present Day Papers. A monthly journal for the presentation of vital and spiritual Christianity, 1, 2, 1914, 37-39.

– Seeing him who is invisible, in: Present Day Papers. A monthly journal for the presentation of vital and spiritual Christianity, 1, 3, 1914, 63-65.

– The inner way, 1, in: Present Day Papers. A monthly journal for the presentation of vital and spiritual Christianity, 1, 3, 1914, 65-68.

– The inner way, 2, in: Present Day Papers. A monthly journal for the presentation of vital and spiritual Christianity, 1, 4, 1914, 93-95.

– Remember Lot's wife, in: Present Day Papers. A monthly journal for the presentation of vital and spiritual Christianity, 1, 5, 1914, 125-126.

– The inner way, 3, in: Present Day Papers. A monthly journal for the presentation of vital and spiritual Christianity, 1, 5, 1914, 125-128.

– "Measures short of war", in: Present Day Papers. A monthly journal for the presentation of vital and spiritual Christianity, 1, 5, 1914, 128.

– The underlying issue of life, in: Present Day Papers. A monthly journal for the presentation of vital and spiritual Christianity, 1, 6, 1914, 157-159.

– The inner way, 4, in: Present Day Papers. A monthly journal for the presentation of vital and spiritual Christianity, 1, 6, 1914, 160-162.

– The new and living way, in: Present Day Papers. A monthly journal for the presentation of vital and spiritual Christianity, 1, 7, 1914, 187-189.

– Bags that wax not cold, in: Present Day Papers. A monthly journal for the presentation of vital and spiritual Christianity, 1, 8, 1914, 218-219.

– The unity of faith, in: Present Day Papers. A monthly journal for the presentation of vital and spiritual Christianity, 1, 8, 1914, 220-222.

– The gift of preaching, in: Present Day Papers. A monthly journal for the presentation of vital and spiritual Christianity, 1, 9, 1914, 252-254.

– Gains in the Christian churches of America in 1910, in: The American Friend, 17, 7, 1910, 99.

– The inner way, 5, in: Present Day Papers. A monthly journal for the presentation of vital and spiritual Christianity, 1, 11, 1914, 311-314.

– The power of prayer, in: Present Day Papers. A monthly journal for the presentation of vital and spiritual Christianity, 1, 10, 1914, 314-317.

– The peace conviction, in: Present Day Papers. A monthly journal for the presentation of vital and spiritual Christianity, 1, 12, 1914, 341-344.

– Godness and efficiency, in: Present Day Papers. A monthly journal for the presentation of vital and spiritual Christianity, 2, 1, 1915, 1-3.

– Scavengers and the kingdom, in: Present Day Papers. A monthly journal for the presentation of vital and spiritual Christianity, 2, 1, 1915, 4-6.

– Waiting on God, in: Present Day Papers. A monthly journal for the presentation of vital and spiritual Christianity, 2, 2, 1915, 35-38.

– The tragedy of false theories, in: Present Day Papers. A monthly journal for the presentation of vital and spiritual Christianity, 2, 2, 1915, 39-41.

– The Sunday revival, in: Present Day Papers. A monthly journal for the presentation of vital and spiritual Christianity, 2, 2, 1915, 43.

– "The beyond is within", in: Present Day Papers. A monthly journal for the presentation of vital and spiritual Christianity, 2, 3, 1915, 69-71.

– The attitude toward the unseen, in: Present Day Papers. A monthly journal for the presentation of vital and spiritual Christianity, 2, 4, 1915, 107-110.

– Otherism, in: Present Day Papers. A monthly journal for the presentation of vital and spiritual Christianity, 2, 5, 1915, 139-140.

– An Apostle of the inner way, in: Present Day Papers. A monthly journal for the presentation of vital and spiritual Christianity, 2, 6, 1915, 167-171.

– The scope and authority of inward light, in: Present Day Papers. A monthly journal for the presentation of vital and spiritual Christianity, 2, 7, 1915, 197-201.

– Ask and ye shall receive, in: Present Day Papers. A monthly journal for the presentation of vital and spiritual Christianity, 2, 7, 1915, 202-203.

– The Psalmist's way, in: Present Day Papers. A monthly journal for the presentation of vital and spiritual Christianity, 2, 8, 1915, 232-234.

– The trail maker, in: Present Day Papers. A monthly journal for the presentation of vital and spiritual Christianity, 2, 8, 1915, 234-236.

– The idiocy of recurrence, in: Present Day Papers. A monthly journal for the presentation of vital and spiritual Christianity, 2, 9, 1915, 261-262.

– Unusual weather, in: Present Day Papers. A monthly journal for the presentation of vital and spiritual Christianity, 2, 9, 1915, 263-264.

– Conservatism and contentment, in: Present Day Papers. A monthly journal for the presentation of vital and spiritual Christianity, 2, 10, 1915, 292-295.

– The idealist and the pure idealist, in: Present Day Papers. A monthly journal for the presentation of vital and spiritual Christianity, 2, 10, 1915, 295-299.

– The strain on religion, in: Present Day Papers. A monthly journal for the presentation of vital and spiritual Christianity, 2, 11, 1915, 321-324.

– The Gospel of the comforter, in: Present Day Papers. A monthly journal for the presentation of vital and spiritual Christianity, 2, 11, 1915, 324-326.

– "As one having authority", in: Present Day Papers. A monthly journal for the presentation of vital and spiritual Christianity, 2, 12, 1915, 351-356.

– Hail and farwell, in: Present Day Papers. A monthly journal for the presentation of vital and spiritual Christianity, 2, 12, 1915, 356-358.

– Christianity - an ideal for the future or a way of life for the present? New York 1916.

– A Quaker's view of Christian unity, in: The South African Ambassador, 1, 4, 1917, 1.

– Christian unity, in: The Friend. A religious, literary, and miscellaneous journal, 57, 6, 1917, 93-94.

– Concerning immortality, in: The Friend. A religious, literary, and miscellaneous journal, 57, 18, 1917, 325-326.

– Concerning immortality, in: The Biblical World, 49, 6, 1917, 339-341.

– St. Paul the hero, New York 1917. New York 1922[2]. New York 1923[3]. New York 1926[4].

– The devotional hour, 11. A religion which does things, in: The Homiletic Review. An international magazine of religion, theology, and philosophy, 75, 1, 1918, 3-4.

– The devotinal hour, 12. Let us be Habakkukeans, in: The Homiletic Review. An international magazine of religion, theology, and philosophy, 75, 2, 1918, 89-90.

– The devotinal hour, 13. "From above", in: The Homiletic Review. An international magazine of religion, theology, and philosophy, 75, 3, 1918, 175-177.

– The devotional hour, 14. That which is not brings to naught that which is, in: The Homiletic Review. An international magazine of religion, theology, and philosophy, 75, 4, 1918, 261-263.

– The devotional hour, 15. Becoming like little children, in: The Homiletic Review. An international magazine of religion, theology, and philosophy, 75, 5, 1918, 347-348.

– The devotional hour, 16. The inner issue in Gethsemane, in: The Homiletic Review. An international magazine of religion, theology, and philosophy, 75, 6, 1918, 433-434.

– The devotional hour, 17. Heart or head, in: The Homiletic Review. An international magazine of religion, theology, and philosophy, 76, 1, 1918, 3-4.

– The devotional hour, 18. The prophet and his tragedies, in: The Homiletic Review. An international magazine of religion, theology, and philosophy, 76, 2, 1918, 89-91.

– The devotional hour, 19. Poured out, in: The Homiletic Review. An international magazine of religion, theology, and philosophy, 76, 3, 1918, 175-176.

– The devotional hour, 20. Days of greater visibility, in: The Homiletic Review. An international magazine of religion, theology, and philosophy, 76, 4, 1918, 261-262.

– The devotional hour, 21. Peace that passes understanding, in: The Homiletic Review. An international magazine of religion, theology, and philosophy, 76, 5, 1918, 347-348.

– The devotional hour, 22. We have seen his star, in: The Homiletic Review. An international magazine of religion, theology, and philosophy, 76, 6, 1918, 433-434.

– Let us be Habakkukeans, in: The Friend. A religious, literary, and miscellaneous journal, 58, 7, 1918, 101-102.

– The essential truth of Christianity, in: The World Tomorrow. A journal looking toward a Christian world, 1, 7, 1918, 158-159.

– The essential truth of Christianity, in: The Friend. A religious, literary, and miscellaneous journal, 58, 31, 1918, 480-481.

– The Quaker conception of the church, New York 1918.

– The Quaker conception of the church, in: The American Friend, 6, 22, 1918, 436-439.

– Two worlds, in: The Homiletic Review. An international magazine of religion, theology, and philosophy, 77, 3, 1919, 175-177.

– Devotional - the search for a refuge, in: The Homiletic Review. An international magazine of religion, theology, and philosophy, 77, 4, 1919, 261-262.

– Devotional things present and things to come, in: The Homiletic Review. An international magazine of religion, theology, and philosophy, 77, 5, 1919, 347-348.

– The moral universe and the individual, in: The Homiletic Review. An international magazine of religion, theology, and philosophy, 77, 6, 1919, 433-435.

– Some new reasons for "loving enemies", in: The Homiletic Review. An international magazine of religion, theology, and philosophy, 78, 1, 1919, 3-5.

– Conquering by inner force, in: The Homiletic Review. An international magazine of religion, theology, and Philosophy, 78, 2, 1919, 89-90.

– The church of the living God, in: The Homiletic Review. An international magazine of religion, theology, and philosophy, 78, 3, 1919, 175-176.

– The nursery of spiritual life, in: The Homiletic Review. An international magazine of religion, theology, and philosophy, 78, 4, 1919, 259-260.

– A long distance call, in: The Homiletic Review. An international magazine of religion, theology, and philosophy, 78, 5, 1919, 345-346.

– Living in the presence of the eternal, in: The Homiletic Review. An international magazine of religion, theology, and philosophy, 78, 6, 1919, 429-430.

– Two types of ministry, in: The Homiletic Review. An international magazine of religion, theology, and philosophy, 79, 1, 1920, 3-4.

– Where the beyond breaks through, in: The Homiletic Review. An international magazine of religion, theology, and philosophy, 79, 2, 1920, 89-91.

– "He came to himself", in: The Homiletic Review. An international magazine of religion, theology, and philosophy, 79, 3, 1920, 175-177.

– Another kind of hero, in: The Homiletic Review. An international magazine of religion, theology, and philosophy, 79, 4, 1920, 261-262.

– The better possession, in: The Homiletic Review. An international magazine of religion, theology, and philosophy, 79, 5, 1920, 347-349.

– What we most want, in: The Homiletic Review. An international magazine of religion, theology, and philosophy, 79, 6, 1920, 433-434.

– The greatest rivalries of life, in: The Homiletic Review. An international magazine of religion, theology, and philosophy, 80, 1, 1920, 3-4.

– Preparation for life's greatest business, in: The Homiletic Review. An international magazine of religion, theology, and philosophy, 80, 2, 1920, 87-89.

– Benediction, in: Christian Century Pulpit, 1, 6, 1920, 4-6.

– The nature and authority of conscience, London 1920.

– Hebreeuwsche Helden, Assen, ca. 1920.

– Het Heldenleven van Paulus, Assen, ca. 1920.

– The remnant, London 1920 (The Christian Revolution Series, 8).

– The religious significance of death, Harrogate 1920.

– Some by-products of life, Washington 1920.

– War and the teaching of Jesus, in: Christian Century, 38, 36, 1921, 9-12.

– The message of Christ to the world today. Notes from an address delivered May 7 at the Baltimore Anniversary Observance, in: The American Friend, 10, 20, 1922, 392-393.

– The religious tendency - Whither? In: The Friends' Intelligencer, 79, 42, 1922, 660-661.

– The experience of religion, in: The World Tomorrow. A journal looking toward a Christian world, 5, 5, 1922, 136-138.

– Making a life, in: Christian Work, 112, 1922, 742-743.

– Baptism and communion, Philadelphia 1922.

– The boy Jesus and his companions, New York 1922. New York 1924[2]. New York 1930[3]. New York 1947[4].

– Burning of the heart, in: Christian Work, 112, 11, 1922, 330.

– The land of the Bible, in: The American Friend, 11, 15, 1923, 275-276.

– Religious foundations. By A. Clutton-Brock, Elihu Grant, PH. D., Prof. L. P. Jacks, Rufus M. Jones, Prof. Eugene W. Lyman, Prof. Francis G. Peabody,

B. Seebohm Rowntree, Dean Willard L. Sperry. Edited by Rufus Jones, New York 1923.

– As one having authority, in: The Homiletic Review. An international magazine of religion, theology, and philosophy, 87, 2, 1924.

– The inner springs of joy: Did you ever stop to think what the elements of joy really are - especially at Christmas time? In: The Adult Bible Class Monthly, 17, 12, 1924, 353-355.

– San Pablo el Heroe, Mexico 1924.

– The story of a boy king, Leeds 1924.

– Divergent religious bodies, in: Peake, A. S. (ed.): The rise of the modern churches, London 1926, 275-288 (An Outline of Christianity, 3).

– Religion and life, Shanghai 1926.

– The life of Christ, Chicago 1926 (Reading with a Purpose, 15).

– New secularism, in: Foreign Missions Conference of North America (ed.): Report of the 43d Annual Meeting of the Conference of Foreign Missions Boards in Canada and in the United States, New York 1926, 88-91.

– The eternal Goodness, in: Newton, Joseph Fort (ed.): My idea of God. A symposium of faith, Boston 1927, 53-65.

– Christmas and the home, in: Children, 2, 12, 1927, 7.

– The world-wide opportunity for a new way of life, in: The Messenger of Peace, 52, 10, 1927, 241-251.

– Building the soul of a people, in: The World Tomorrow. A journal looking toward a Christian world, 10, 7, 1927, 307-308.

– Religious life in China, in: The Friend. A religious and literary journal, 62, 1, 1927, 1-3.

– Christianity and secular civilization, New York 1928.

– What salvation can the church offer today? In: The Christian Century. An undenominational journal, 45, 6, 1928, 171-172.

– The new quest, in: The Institution Bulletin, Newton Centre, Mass., Andover Newton Theological School, 20, 6, 1928, 7-11.

– Our Christian task in a materialistic world, London 1928 (The Jerusalem Meeting of the International Missionary).

– The nursery of souls, in: Pound, James Presley (ed.): Voices of the age, New York 1929, 145-158.

– The way of wonder, in: Listener, 2, 37, 1929, 415.

– The spiritual adventure, in: Chicago Theological Seminary Register, 19, 1, 1929, 23-27.

– The power of prayer, London 1929.

– Immortality, in: Strong, Sydney Dix (ed.): We believe in immortality. Affirmations by one hundred men and women, New York 1929, 124-126.

– The spirit, in: Jones, Rufus Matthew; Shailer, Mathews; Tittle, Ernst; McConnell, Francis; Sapir, Edward (ed.): Religious life, New York 1929, 87-108 (Man and His World, 11).

– All is not right with the world, in: Christian Century. A journal of religion, 47, 51, 1930, 1556-1557.

– What it means to pray, in: Van Dusen, Henry P. (ed.): Ventures in belief. Christian convictions for a day of uncertainty, New York 1930, 163-180.

– The eternal Gospel, in: Methodist Review. Bimonthly, 113, 4, 1930, 481-487.

– The life beyond, in: The Christian Advocate, 105, 16, 1930, 490-491.

– A primer of Christian faith for a New Age, n.p., 1930. Reprint n.p., 1932.

– What I believe - about prayer, in: Dusen, Henry P. Van (ed.): Ventures in belief. Christian convictions for a day of uncertainty, New York 1930, 159-180.

– What's the universe like? In: The Intercollegian, 48, 3, 1931, 177-178.

– Looking ahead on the cosmic calendar, in: The Intercollegian, 48, 4, 1931, 213-214, 224.

– "Take heed to thyself", in: The Westminster Leader, 4, 4, 1931, 1-2.

– Pathways to the reality of God, New York 1931. New York 1932[2]. Los Angeles 1936 (American Brotherhood for the Blinds, vol. 2).

– The transfigured life, in: Young Men's Christian Associations. World Committee (ed.): Youth's adventure with God. Being the official report of the third world assembly of Y.M.C.A. workers with boys, the first world Y.M.C.A. assembly of young men, and the twentieth world's conference of the Y.M.C.A., July 27th - August 2nd, and August 4th - 9th, 1931, London 1931, 190-196.

– Preparing for life's greatest business, in: Christian Endeavor World, 48, 11, 1932, 14.

– "Light lives". A sermon preached in Trinity Church, Boston, Sunday, December 11th, 1932, Boston 1932.

– The heart of Christianity, in: The Friend. A religious and literary journal, 90, 29, 1932, 609-611.

– The issues of the soul, in: The Friend. A religious and literary journal, 90, 49, 1932, 1035-1036.

– The issues of soul, in: Edwards, Boyd; Ingalls, Harold (ed.): Religion in the preparatory schools. The proceedings of the National Conference of Preparatory School Masters, held at Atlantic City, N. J., October 7-9, New York 1932, 13-15.

– Striking a vein of reality, in: Newton, Joseph Fort (ed.): If I had only one sermon to prepare, New York 1932, 205-208.

– A preface to Christian faith in a New Age, New York 1932. London 1932[2].

– Road-makers for the new day, in: Searle, Robert Wyckoff; Bowers, Frederick A. (ed.): Contemporary religious thinking. Seventeen sermons on the Church's responsibilities in the period just ahead, New York 1933, 117-124.

– Evangelism for the whole man, in: Evangelism heralds of the good news, in: The Annual College of Preachers, Evanston, 3, 1933, 39-43.

– What the philosophers and scientists are saying, in: Christian Education, 17, 1, 1933, 58-59.

– Religion. A mutual and reciprocal correspondence between God and man, in: Religion in Life, 3, 1, 1934, 13-23.

– Eine große Erweckung, in: Theologische Blätter, 13, 2, 1934, 33-43.

– Re-thinking religious liberalism. The fourth unification address on the Arthur Emmons Pearson Foundation, Boston 1935.

– "Die Gesinnung Christi in unserer Zeit", in: Der Quäker. Monatshefte der deutschen Freunde, 13, 4, 1936, 97-100.

– Some problems of life, Nashville 1937. London 1937[2].

– A great spiritual diary, in: Commonweal. A weekly review of literature, the arts and public affairs, 26, 8, 1937, 210-211.

– The double search. Studies in atonement and prayer, Philadelphia, ca. 1937. Reprint Richmond 1975.

– The eternal Gospel, New York 1938. London 1938[2].

– Building the new temples, in: Cathedral Monthly, 1, 1, 1938, 4-7.

– Church unity, in: The Friend. A religious and literary journal, 112, 3, 1939, 37-39.

– Back to the springs and sources of life, in: World Wide Listener, 2, 11, 1939.

– "Many members but one body". A plea for the spirit of unity among Christians, in: London Friend. The Quaker weekly journal, 98, 13, 1940, 189-191.

– Low visibility, in: The Church Woman, 6, 10, 1940, 10-12.

– Jones, Rufus Mattew; Carver, George Washington; Clark, Glenn; Lester, Muriel: God's minute men, St. Paul 1940.

– They mend the heart, in: Atlantic Monthly, 165, 3, 1940, 332-337.

– The spirit of Christmas, in: The Christian Leader, 123, 47, 1941, 969-970.

– The church as an organ of social ideals, in: Pennsylvania University Bicentennial Conference. Religion and the modern world, Philadelphia 1941, 109-118.

– A call to persons of good will, in: World Affairs, 104, 9, 1941, 138.

– Christ's philosopher, in: Protestant Digest, 3, 2/3, 1941, 43-46.

– Spirit in man, London 1941. Reprint Berkeley 1963.

– The shepherd who missed the manger, New York 1941. Philadelphia 1948[2]. Philadelphia 1958[3].

– Begin with the church! 15. How shall the Christian church prepare for the new world order? In: Christian Century. Published weekly, 59, 20, 1942, 659-661.

– A great experiment, in: Survey Graphic. Magazine of social interpretation, 31, 8, 1942, 354-355.

– A call to persons of good will, n.p., 1942.

– A great experiment, Philadelphia 1942.

– What I acquired at play, in: Recreation, 36, 1, 1943, 548-553.

– Vom Hirten, der nicht zur Krippe gelangte, in: Kirchenblatt, 86, 52, 1943, 13-16; 87, 1, 1944, 4-5.

– Beyond the old frontiers, in: The American Pulpit Series, 8. Containing sermons by Joseph R. Sizoo, Alonzo Willard Fortune, Daniel A. Poling, Rufus M. Jones, Richard C. Raines, Andrew W. Blackwoood, Allan A. Hunter, Ralph S. Cushman, New York 1945, 46-55.

– Old Testament heroes, London 1947.

– Claim everything, in: Best sermons, New York 1947, 33-34.

– What the modern man can believe, in: The Atlantic, 180, 5, 1947, 88-93.

– Jones, Rufus Matthew (ed.): The church, the Gospel, and war, New York 1948. New York 1971² (i.e. 1972) (The Garland Library of War and Peace).

– A call to a new installment of heroic spirit, Winthrop 1948.

– Le dynamisme de la foi, Genève 1949.

– Light can be had, in: Rhoades, Winfried (ed.): To know God better, New York 1958, 60.

– I must become organized, in: Rhoades, Winfried (ed.): To know God better, New York 1958, 63.

– Increasing capacity, in: Rhoades, Winfried (ed.): To know God better, New York 1958, 139.

– Die Kirche darf die Wahrheit nicht mißachten, in: Gressel, Hans; Kloppenburg, Heinz (ed.): Versöhnung und Friede. 50 Jahre Internationaler Versöhnungsbund (3. August 1964), Dortmund 1964, 74.

Missionary Work

– The turning point in Friends' Missionary World, in: The American Friend, 14, 17, 1907, 259.

– A new epoch in mission work, in: The American Friend, 16, 50, 1909, 791-792.

– The great missionary conference, in: The American Friend, 17, 27, 1910, 419.

– A sense of mission, in: The American Friend, 18, 50, 1911, 791.

– What the missionaries have been teaching the church, in: Friends' Intelligencer, 70, 42, 1913, 659-660.

– The birth of Friends foreign mission work, in: The American Friend, 5, 28, 1917, 544-545.

– Mission and service, in: The American Friend, 10, 27, 1922, 525.

– Secular civilisation and the Christian task, in: The Christian life and message in relation to non-christian systems, New York 1928, 284-338 (Report of the Jerusalem Meeting of the International Missionary Council March 24th. - April 8th., 1928, 1).

– Consciousness of a unique mission, in: Friends' Intelligencer, 90, 21, 1933, 405-406.

– The background and the objectives of foreign missions 1933, in: Crozer Quarterly, 10, 4, 1933, 129-144.

– The background and the objectives of foreign missions 1933. Reprinted from the Crozer Quarterly, n.p., 1933.

– Consciousness of a unique mission, in: The Friend. A religious and literary journal, 91, 25, 1933, 549-550.

– The new day in mission, in: The American Friend, 21, 30, 1933, 416-417.

– The background and the objectives of protestant foreign missions, in: Petty, Orville A. (ed.): China, New York 1933, xi-xxiii (Laymen's Foreign Missionary Inquiry. Regional Reports of the Commission of Appraisal. Supplementary Series, 2, 1).

– The work of missions today, in: The Friend. A religious and literary journal, 110, 6, 1936, 83-84.

– Message and mission of Friends today. Address broadcast in Europe from the Friends World Conference on Sunday, September 5th, through the courtesy of the British Broadcasting Corporation, in: Friends' Intelligencer, 94, 38, 1937, 631-633.

– Our mission unchanged, in: Fellowship, 5, 10, 1939, 14.

– A call to mission, in: The Friend. The Quaker weekly journal, 101, 45, 1943, 733-734.

Quakerism & Quaker Issues

– The Society of Friends, in: Kingsbury, Henry D. (ed.): Illustrated history of
Kennebec County, Maine: 1625-1799-1892, New York 1892, 269-296.

– Historical sketch of Baltimore Yearly Meeting, in: The American Friend, 8,
46, 1901, 1087-1088.

– The message of Quakerism. Two Addresses, London 1901.

– The ministry of ordinary people, Leeds, ca. 1905 (1905 Committee of Yorkshire Quarterly Meeting of the Society of Friends).

– A religion which does things, Leeds, ca. 1905 (1905 Committee of Yorkshire Quarterly Meeting of the Society of Friends).

– An everyday saint, Leeds, ca. 1905 (1905 Committee of Yorkshire Quarterly
Meeting of the Society of Friends).

– Diversions and recreations. Reprinted from "Practical Christianity", Hull,
ca. 1905 (Yorkshire 1905 Committee of Yorkshire Quarterly Meeting of the
Society of Friends).

– The place of the home in civilisation, Hull, ca. 1905 (1905 Committee of
Yorkshire Quarterly Meeting of the Society of Friends).

– The real presence of God, Hull, ca. 1905 (1905 Committee of Yorkshire
Quarterly Meeting of the Society of Friends).

– Jones, Rufus; Thomas, Richard H.: The objects of public worship, Malton
ca. 1905 (1905 Committee of Yorkshire Quarterly Meeting of the Society of
Friends).

– A simple religion, Hull 1905 (1905 Committee of Yorkshire Quarterly
Meeting of the Society of Friends).

– The most serious scepticism, Leeds, ca. 1905 (1905 Committee of Yorkshire
Quarterly Meeting of the Society of Friends).

– Quick gains and far values, Leeds, ca. 1905 (1905 Committee of Yorkshire
Quarterly Meeting of the Society of Friends). Reprint Philadelphia 1922
(Pennsbury Leaflet, 6).

– The test of a church, Leeds, ca. 1905 (1905 Committee of Yorkshire Quarterly Meeting of the Society of Friends).

– The Gospel of the kingdom, Leeds, ca. 1905 (1905 Committee of Yorkshire Quarterly Meeting of the Society of Friends).

– Prayer, Hull, ca. 1905 (1905 Committee of Yorkshire Quarterly Meeting of the Society of Friends).

– Our social task and the life which it demands, n.p., ca. 1905 (1905 Committee of Yorkshire Quarterly Meeting).

– The peace of the home in civilization, Leeds, ca. 1905 (1905 Committee of Yorkshire Quarterly Meeting of the Society of Friends).

– A very early call, in: The Friend. A religious, literary, and miscellaneous journal, 46, 12, 1906, 182.

– Either - or, in: The Friend. A religious, literary, and miscellaneous journal, 47, 52, 1906, 883.

– Rufus M. Jones on the progress of English Quakerism, in: The Friend. A religious, literary, and miscellaneous journal, 47, 42, 1906, 708.

– Some thoughts on fellowship, in: The British Friend. A religious and literary journal, written from the standpoint of the Society of Friends, 15, 2, 1906, 49-50.

– Quakerism and the simple life, in: Friends' Intelligencer, 63, 13, 1906, 197.

– Rufus M. Jones on the Five Years Meeting and London Yearly Meeting, in: The Friend. A religious, literary, and miscellaneous journal, 47, 27, 1906, 441-442.

– Quakerism and the simple life, London 1906.

– Vicariousness, in: The Friend. A religious, literary, and miscellaneous journal, 47, 49, 1906, 818-819.

– Speaking without tongues, in: The American Friend, 14, 3, 1907, 36.

– A serious call, in: The American Friend, 14, 4, 1907, 51-52.

– An ordinary saint, in: The American Friend, 14, 5, 1907, 67.

– Afraid of fading ink, in: The American Friend, 14, 2, 1907, 19.

– Some by-products of life, in: The American Friend, 14, 6, 1907, 83-84.

– Campaigns of ignorance, in: The American Friend, 14, 16, 1907, 243.

– A woman of great faith, in: The American Friend, 14, 23, 1907, 355.

– A leader in the revival Movement, in: The American Friend, 14, 32, 1907, 499-500.

– One more serious call, in: The American Friend, 14, 8, 1907, 115-116.

– An ordinary saint, in: The American Friend, 14, 10, 1907, 147.

– Does our religion make any difference? In: The American Friend, 14, 11, 1907, 163.

– The life of four dimensions, in: The American Friend, 14, 14, 1907, 211.

– Quick gains and fair values, in: The American Friend, 14, 24, 1907, 371.

– Two types of optimism, in: The American Friend, 14, 25, 1907, 387-388.

– Local meetings on ministry and oversight, in: The American Friend, 14, 26, 1907, 403-404.

– New England Yearly Meeting, in: The American Friend, 14, 27, 1907, 419-420.

– Friends in Canada, in: The American Friend, 14, 28, 1907, 435-436.

– The peril of deadness, in: The American Friend, 14, 29, 1907, 451-452.

– The need of thinking, in: The American Friend, 14, 30, 1907, 467.

– How the soil gets its holiday, in: The American Friend, 14, 31, 1907, 483-484.

– The temperance outlook, in: The American Friend, 14, 42, 1907, 663-665.

– The Five Years Meeting - a review, in: The American Friend, 14, 44, 1907, 695-696.

– The good fight for faith, in: The American Friend, 14, 45, 1907, 715.

– Daily tragedies, in: The American Friend, 14, 46, 1907, 731.

– What makes a person free? In: The American Friend, 14, 47, 1907, 747.

– "Truth is the inward parts", in: The American Friend, 14, 48, 1907, 763.

– What saves a person? In: The American Friend, 14, 50, 1907, 795.

– Let us try to be as good people say we are, in: The American Friend, 14, 51, 1907, 811.

– A backward look, in: The American Friend, 15, 1, 1908, 3-4.

– Shall we make 1908 a great year? In: The American Friend, 15, 2, 1908, 19.

– Oh, for wings like a dove, in: The American Friend, 15, 4, 1908, 51.

– The call for prophets, in: The American Friend, 15, 5, 1908, 67.

– The new Muncie "Meeting-House", in: The American Friend, 15, 8, 1908, 120.

– Flabbiness, in: The American Friend, 15, 15, 1908, 227.

– High time to wake, in: The American Friend, 15, 17, 1908, 259-260.

– The endless life, in: The American Friend, 15, 19, 1908, 291.

– Fellowship in suffering, in: The American Friend, 15, 1908, 307.

– Enduring the weather, in: The American Friend, 15, 21, 1908, 323.

– Preparing for a Yearly Meeting, in: The American Friend, 15, 22, 1908, 339.

– Running with horses, in: The American Friend, 15, 23, 1908, 355,

– London Yearly Meeting in Birmingham, in: The American Friend, 15, 25, 1908, 387-388.

– Two important books, in: The American Friend, 15, 27, 1908, 419-420.

– What is missing? In: The American Friend, 15, 28, 1908, 435.

– The coming of woman, in: The American Friend, 15, 29, 1908, 451-452.

– The responsibilities of the keys, in: The American Friend, 15, 30, 1908, 467.

– In high places, in: The American Friend, 15, 36, 1908, 567-568.

– A day in Worms, in: The American Friend, 15, 38, 1908, 599-600.

– The call to life and action, in: The American Friend, 15, 39, 1908, 615-616.

– English and American Quakerism, in: The American Friend, 15, 40, 1908, 631-632.

– Two hundred and twenty-five years after, in: The American Friend, 15, 41, 1908, 647.

– Indifferentism, in: The American Friend, 15, 42, 1908, 663.

– A religion that sweetens, in: The American Friend, 15, 44, 1908, 695.

– The glory of going on, 1, in: The American Friend, 15, 48, 1908, 759-760.

– The glory of going on, 2, in: The American Friend, 15, 49, 1908, 775-776.

– The hero as invalid, in: The American Friend, 15, 50, 1908, 791.

– Why could not we cast him out? In: The American Friend, 15, 11, 1908, 163.

– Where now is thy God? In: The American Friend, 15, 52, 1908, 823-824.

– Called to be saints, in: The American Friend, 15, 53, 1908, 839.

– Divine worship the heart of our religion, in: Friends' Fellowship Papers, 2, 5, 1908, 133-143.

– The friendly social task, in: Friends' Intelligencer, 65, 25, 1908, 391.

– Quakerism. A religion of life. London 1908. London 1908[2]. London 1912[3] (Swarthmore Lecture, 1, 1908).

– The abundant life, London 1908.

– Yorkshire week-end quarterly meeting at Scarborough, in: The Friend. A religious, literary, and miscellaneous journal, 48, 30, 1908, 494-495.

– English and American Quakerism, in: The Friend. A religious, literary, and miscellaneous journal, 48, 42, 1908, 697-698.

– The evangelical note, in: The Friend. A religious, literary, and miscellaneous journal, 48, 14, 1908, 211-212.

– Quakerism: A religion of life. "Swarthmore Lecture" by Rufus Jones, in: The Friend. A religious, literary, and miscellaneous journal, 48, 21, 1908, 326-328.

– The realm of faith, in: The American Friend, 16, 2, 1909, 19.

– Let us pray, in: The American Friend, 16, 5, 1909, 67-68.

– Christ's highest good, in: The American Friend, 16, 6, 1909, 83.

– The consecrated life, in: The American Friend, 16, 7, 1909, 99-100.

– An everyday heroine, in: The American Friend, 16, 8, 1909, 115-116.

– How a little boy was chosen king, in: The American Friend, 16, 6, 1909, 84-86.

– How a boy cheated his brother, in: The American Friend, 16, 10, 1909, 148-149.

– Becoming a castaway, in: The American Friend, 16, 11, 1909, 163.

– Work as an agency of enlargement, in: The American Friend, 16, 12, 1909, 179.

– Religion as beauty of soul, in: The American Friend, 16, 14, 1909, 211.

– The work of ministry and oversight, in: The American Friend, 16, 15, 1909, 227.

– The cultivation of patience, in: The American Friend, 16, 17, 1909, 259.

– The larger outlook, in: The American Friend, 16, 18, 1909, 275.

– How a boy killed a giant, in: The American Friend, 16, 18, 1909, 277-278.

– Spiritual guidance, in: The American Friend, 16, 23, 1909, 355-356.

– London Yearly Meeting, 1909, in: The American Friend, 16, 24, 1909, 371-372.

– What do we need? In: The American Friend, 16, 25, 1909, 387.

– The story of a beautiful friendship, in: The American Friend, 16, 25, 1909, 388-389.

– New England Yearly Meeting, in: The American Friend, 16, 27, 1909, 419-420.

– The organ of balance, in: The American Friend, 16, 28, 1909, 435.

– Facts, in: The American Friend, 16, 29, 1909, 451.

– "Clothes thyself in gladness", in: The American Friend, 16, 30, 1909, 467.

– Keep in the current of Life, in: The American Friend, 16, 33, 1909, 519.

– Trusting the captain, in: The American Friend, 16, 34, 1909, 535.

– More truth to be discovered, in: The American Friend, 16, 35, 1909, 551.

– Making ministers, in: The American Friend, 16, 36, 1909, 567.

– The minister and some of his practical questions, in: The American Friend, 16, 37, 1909, 583.

– Working for a spiritual guide, in: The American Friend, 16, 38, 1909, 599.

– Pleasure or consecration? In: The American Friend, 16, 40, 1909, 631-632.

– The value of anniversaries, in: The American Friend, 16, 41, 1909, 647.

– As a hen gathereth, in: The American Friend, 16, 42, 1909, 663.

– Living in the presence of the eternal, in: The American Friend, 16, 43, 1909, 679.

– A word for the times, in: The American Friend, 16, 44, 1909, 695-696.

– Baltimore Yearly Meeting, in: The American Friend, 16, 47, 1909, 743-744.

– A Friend of the nineteenth century, in: The American Friend, 16, 51, 1909, 807-808.

– The two stars, in: The American Friend, 16, 52, 1909, 823.

– The value of anniversaries, in: Friends' Intelligencer, 66, 44, 1909, 682.

– Little book of selections from the children of the light, London 1909 (The Religion of Life Series).

– The possibility of a new event. Or, the problem of freedom in willing, in: The Friends' Quarterly Examiner. A Religious, social and miscellaneous review, 43, 1, 1909, 33-45.

– Story of the builder, in: The American Friend, 17, 1, 1910, 5-6.

– Story of the great boat, in: The American Friend, 17, 5, 1910, 69-70.

– Story of a great rain and rainbow, in: The American Friend, 17, 10, 1910, 149-150.

– Story of a boy who became a great leader, in: The American Friend, 17, 14, 1910, 212-213.

– Fundamentals of liberal and orthodox Friends, in: The American Friend, 17, 16, 1910, 246-247;

– The group is the unit, in: Friends' Intelligencer, 67, 28, 1910, 445.

– In the grip of the snow, in: The American Friend, 17, 1, 1910, 3.

– What difference does it make? In: The American Friend, 17, 2, 1910, 19.

– In the whirl of controversy, in: The American Friend, 17, 3, 1910, 35.

– The place of God, in: The American Friend, 17, 4, 1910, 51.

– The name, in: The American Friend, 17, 5, 1910, 67-68.

– A week-day religion, in: The American Friend, 17, 6, 1910, 83.

– Separations, in: The American Friend, 17, 8, 1910, 115.

– Quakers in public live and service, in: The American Friend, 17, 10, 1910, 147.

– In the presence of enemies, in: The American Friend, 17, 12, 1910, 179.

– What we want to accomplish, in: The American Friend, 17, 13, 1910, 195-196.

– "Love can never lose it's own", in: The American Friend, 17, 15, 1910, 227.

– Is Quakerism worth while? In: The American Friend, 17, 16, 1910, 243.

– A great confession of faith, in: The American Friend, 17, 17, 1910, 259-260.

– The devotional point of view, in: The American Friend, 17, 18, 1910, 275.

– Of such is the Kingdom, in: The American Friend, 17, 19, 1910, 291.

– The battle is on, in: The American Friend, 17, 21, 1910, 323-324.

– An admirable minute, in: The American Friend, 17, 22, 1910, 339.

– "The new and living way", in: The American Friend, 17, 23, 1910, 355-356.

– A lesson from our past, in: The American Friend, 17, 25, 1910, 387-388.

– The easy ministry, in: The American Friend, 17, 28, 1910, 435.

– The return to the cross, in: The American Friend, 17, 29, 1910, 451.

– Growing old with God, in: The American Friend, 17, 30, 1910, 467.

– On being young, in: The American Friend, 17, 31, 1910, 483.

– Unloading dangerous freight, in: The American Friend, 17, 32, 1910, 499-500.

– Broken windows, in: The American Friend, 17, 33, 1910, 519.

– If Christ came, in: The American Friend, 17, 34, 1910, 535.

– A religion of depth, in: The American Friend, 17, 38, 1910, 599.

– Keep the young people, in: The American Friend, 17, 39, 1910, 615.

– Burning and shining, in: The American Friend, 17, 41, 1910, 647.

– The value of tested experience, in: The American Friend, 17, 43, 1910, 679.

– The new Quakerism, in: The American Friend, 17, 44, 1910, 695.

– Some subtle forms of scepticism, in: The American Friend, 17, 45, 1910, 711-712.

– From the sidelines, in: The American Friend, 17, 47, 1910, 743-744.

– Quakerism a religion of life, in: The American Friend, 17, 49, 1910, 775-777.

– Two religious attitudes, in: The American Friend, 17, 50, 1910, 791.

– Forward or backward, in: The American Friend, 18, 2, 1911, 19.

– The word became flesh, in: The American Friend, 18, 3, 1911, 35.

– The gains of peace, in: The American Friend, 18, 4, 1911, 51.

– A great coming anniversary, in: The American Friend, 18, 9, 1911, 131.

– The fact of vicarious suffering, in: The American Friend, 18, 10, 1911, 147-148.

– How shall we safeguard the truth? In: The American Friend, 18, 11, 1911, 163.

– Worship, in: The American Friend, 18, 12, 1911, 179.

– "With the spirit and the understanding also", in: The American Friend, 18, 13, 1911, 195.

– Faith as a way of life, in: The American Friend, 18, 14, 1911, 211-212.

– How a beautiful girl became a Queen and saved her people, in: The American Friend, 18, 14, 1911, 214-215.

– Practical sacrifices, in: The American Friend, 18, 15, 1911, 227.

– "Individual faithfulness", in: The American Friend, 18, 16, 1911, 243.

– Spiritual preaching, in: The American Friend, 18, 17, 1911, 259.

– How a boy lost his home, became great, and was thrown into a Lion's den, in: The American Friend, 18, 18, 1911, 278.

– Edward Grubb on the personality of God, in: The American Friend, 18, 20, 1911, 307-308.

– The story of a garden, in: The American Friend, 18, 21, 1911, 326-327.

– The center of our faith, in: The American Friend, 18, 22, 1911, 339.

– Turning the hearts of the fathers to the children, in: The American Friend, 18, 23, 1911, 355-356.

– Empty shells, in: The American Friend, 18, 24, 1911, 371-372.

– The early history of England Yearly Meeting, in: The American Friend, 18, 26, 1911, 406-407.

– The early history of New England Yearly Meeting, in: The American Friend, 18, 27, 1911, 422-423.

– At the city of the soul, in: The American Friend, 18, 28, 1911, 435-436.

– The decline in New England, in: The American Friend, 18, 33, 1911, 519-520.

– The strength of custom, in: The American Friend, 18, 34, 1911, 535-536.

– The unity of faith, in: The American Friend, 18, 37, 1911, 583.

– Young Friends in council, in: The American Friend, 18, 38, 1911, 599-600.

– The pilot of our ship, in: The American Friend, 18, 39, 1911, 615-616.

– A plea for spiritual homes, in: The American Friend, 18, 40, 1911, 631-632.

– The way of faith, in: The American Friend, 18, 43, 1911, 679.

– The center of our faith, in: The American Friend, 18, 44, 1911, 695-696.

– One of our main hindrances, in: The American Friend, 18, 46, 1911, 727.

– Form and life, in: The American Friend, 18, 47, 1911, 743-744.

– The yoke, in: The American Friend, 18, 48, 1911, 759-760.

– Shall we have a revival? In: The American Friend, 18, 49, 1911, 775-776.

– Worship. Richmond 1911;

– The first Quaker in America, in: Bulletin of Friends' Historical Society of Philadelphia, 4, 1, 1911, 58-59.

– "Individual faithfulness", in: Friends' Intelligencer, 68, 17, 1911, 261.

– The supreme questions, in: British Friend. A religious and literary journal, written from the standpoint of the Society of Friends, 20, 9, 1911, 241-242.

– Moral ideals and practical tasks, in: The Friend. A religious, literary, and miscellaneous journal, 51, 44, 1911, 706-707.

– The pilot of our ship, in: The Friend. A religious, literary, and miscellaneous journal, 51, 42, 1911, 678-679.

– Rufus M. Jones on Swanwick, in: The Friend. A religious, literary, and miscellaneous journal, 51, 40, 1911, 650-651.

– The early history of New England Yearly Meeting, in: Two hundred and fiftieth anniversary of the beginning of New England Yearly Meeting of Friends held at Moses Brown School, Providence, R. I. Sixth Month, 24th, 1911, n.p., 1911, 11-19.

– Jones, Rufus Matthew; Sharpless, Isaac; Gummere, Amelia: The Quakers in the American colonies, London 1911. Reprint London 1923. Reprint New York 1962. Reprint New York, ca. 1966 (The Quaker History Series, 4).

– Two conceptions of God, in: The Friends' Quarterly Examiner A religious, social and miscellaneous review, 46, 1912, 107-118.

– Out west: The prospects, in: The Friend. A religious, literary, and miscellaneous journal, 52, 39, 1912, 627-628.

– The Five Years Meeting, in: The Friend. A religious, literary, and miscellaneous journal, 52, 42, 1912, 677-678.

– Worship. Preparation, in: The Friend. A religious, literary, and miscellaneous journal, 52, 14, 1912, 211-212.

– The fusing of the group in worship, in: The Friend. A religious, literary, and miscellaneous journal, 52, 15, 1912, 224-225.

– The Five Years Meeting of American Friends, in: The Friend. A religious, literary, and miscellaneous journal, 52, 46, 1912, 745-746.

– Our real task, in: The American Friend, 19, 1, 1912, 2-3.

– Backward and forward, in: The American Friend, 19, 2, 1912, 19-20.

– These sheep, what have they done? In: The American Friend, 19, 3, 1912, 35.

– Two kinds of appeal, in: The American Friend, 19, 4, 1912, 51-52.

– A matter of emphasis, in: The American Friend, 19, 5, 1912, 67-68.

– The Cambridge journal of George Fox, in: The American Friend, 19, 7, 1912, 99-100.

– The central act of religion, in: The American Friend, 19, 8, 1912, 115-116.

– Preparation for worship, in: The American Friend, 19, 9, 1912, 130-131.

– The fusing of the group in worship, in: The American Friend, 19, 10, 1912, 147-148.

– What is orthodox? In: The American Friend, 19, 11, 1912, 163-164.

– The long slope, in: The American Friend, 19, 12, 1912, 179-180.

– The ministry which strikes the average, in: The American Friend, 19, 14, 1912, 211-212.

– The miracle again, in: The American Friend, 19, 16, 1912, 243.

– Heroism in disaster, in: The American Friend, 19, 17, 1912, 259-260.

– Where the trouble lies, in: The American Friend, 19, 18, 1912, 275-276.

– "The burden of the valley of vision", in: The American Friend, 19, 19, 1912, 291-292.

– What has been happening in England? In: The American Friend, 19, 20, 1912, 307-308.

– Our social task and the type of life which it demands, in: The American Friend, 19, 21, 1912, 323-324.

– Contemporary faith, in: The American Friend, 19, 22, 1912, 339-340.

– The cost of the tower, in: The American Friend, 19, 23, 1912, 355-356.

– London Yearly Meeting, 1912, in: The American Friend, 19, 25, 1912, 387-388.

– Modern Gallios, in: The American Friend, 19, 26, 1912, 403-404.

– Let us cultivate confidence, in: The American Friend, 19, 27, 1912, 419.

– New England Yearly Meeting, in: The American Friend, 19, 28, 1912, 435-436.

– Quakerism and social service, in: The American Friend, 19, 30, 1912, 467.

– An ancient that which is spiritual, in: The American Friend, 19, 34, 1912, 535-536.

– Getting the higher point of view, in: The American Friend, 19, 35, 1912, 550.

– The tragedy of ruts, in: The American Friend, 19, 36, 1912, 567.

– Among the peaks, in: The American Friend, 19, 38, 1912, 599-600.

– Where the world is in the making, in: The American Friend, 19, 39, 1912, 615-616.

– A Five-Years Meeting forecast, in: The American Friend, 19, 40, 1912, 631-632.

– Wanting, in: The American Friend, 19, 41, 1912, 647-648.

– The whole costs no more than a half, in: The American Friend, 19, 42, 1912, 663.

– The Five-Years Meeting of 1912, in: The American Friend, 19, 44, 1912, 695-696.

– The twilight zones, in: The American Friend, 19, 45, 1912, 711-712.

– The faith by which we live, in: The American Friend, 19, 47, 1912, 743-744. Seeing both sides, in: The American Friend, 19, 48, 1912, 759-760.

– In spirit and in truth, in: The American Friend, 19, 51, 1912, 807-808.

– What a man's hand is to a man, in: The Friend. A religious, literary, and miscellaneous journal, 53, 38, 1913, 611-612.

– The Quaker peace testimony, in: The Friend. A religious, literary, and miscellaneous journal, 54, 43, 1914, 774-776.

– The power of prayer, in: The Friend. A religious, literary, and miscellaneous journal, 54, 48, 1914, 863-864.

– The use of group-silence in worship, in: Present Day Papers. A monthly journal for the presentation of vital and spiritual Christianity, 1, 4, 1914, 95-98.

– Is it essential to preserve the Society of Friends? In: Present Day Papers. A monthly journal for the presentation of vital and spiritual Christianity, 1, 7, 1914, 189-191.

– Spiritual reformers in the 16th and 17th centuries, London 1914. Reprint London 1928. Reprint New York 1944. Reprint Beacon Hill 1959. Reprint Gloucester 1971 (The Quaker History Series, 2). Reprint Belle Fourche 1998.

– The Quaker peace-testimony, in: Present Day Papers. A monthly journal for the presentation of vital and spiritual Christianity, 1, 10, 1914, 279-282.

– Is it essential to preserve the Society of Friends? In: The Friend. A religious, literary, and miscellaneous journal, 54, 30, 1914, 540-542.

– The Quakers peace position, Richmond 1915.

– Social service and field activities, in: The American Friend, 3, 48, 1915, 760-762.

– The scope and authority of inward light, in: The Friend. A religious, literary, and miscellaneous journal, 55, 29, 1915, 550-552.

– "The beyond is within", in: The Friend. A religious, literary, and miscellaneous journal, 55, 13, 1915, 231-232.

– The Quakers peace position, in: The Survey, 34, 4, 1915, 22-23.

– The tragedy of false theories, in: The Friend. A religious, literary, and miscellaneous journal, 55, 7, 1915, 113-114.

– The spiritual mission of Quakerism, in: Present Day Papers. A monthly journal for the presentation of vital and spiritual Christianity, 2, 5, 1915, 133-138.

– The inner life, New York 1916. New York 1917[2]. New York 1920[3]. New York 1922[4]. New York 1923[5]. New York 1929[6].

– Hail and farwell, in: Westonian, 22, 1, 1916, 25-27.

– A more excellent way, London 1916 (Fellowship Papers). Philadelphia 1921[2].

– Poured out, in: The Friend. A religious, literary, and miscellaneous journal, 56, 17, 1916, 283-284.

– Concerning humility, in: The Friend. A religious, literary, and miscellaneous journal, 56, 29, 1916, 555-556.

– Serving the nation, in: The Friend. A religious, literary, and miscellaneous journal, 56, 27, 1916, 517-518.

– The plumb-line, in: The Friend. A religious, literary, and miscellaneous journal, 56, 47, 1916, 911-913.

– Our contribution, in: The Friend. A religious, literary, and miscellaneous journal, 56, 3, 1916, 27-29.

– The parable of vicarious suffering, in: The Friend. A religious, literary, and miscellaneous journal, 56, 7, 1916, 89-90.

– The Quakers, in: Platner, John Winthorp; Fenn, William W.; Horr, George Edwin; Jones, Rufus Matthew, Hodges, George; Huntington, William Edwards; Adams, John Coleman; Worcester, William Loring: The religious history of New England. King's Chapel Lectures, Cambridge 1917, 177-201.

– The crisis for English Quakerism, in: Westonian, 23, 1, 1917, 14-17.

– A religion which does things, in: The Friend. A religious, literary, and miscellaneous journal, 57, 51, 1917, 961-962.

– The fact of must, in: The Friend. A religious, literary, and miscellaneous journal, 57, 26, 1917, 503-504.

– Finding the pulse, in: The Friend. A religious, literary, and miscellaneous journal, 57, 33, 1917, 628-629.

– Another kind of famine, in: The Friend. A religious, literary, and miscellaneous journal, 57, 29, 1917, 557-558.

– Truth in the inward parts, in: The Friend. A religious, literary, and miscellaneous journal, 57, 40, 1917, 755-756.

– The Meaning of obligation, in: The World Tomorrow. A journal looking toward a Christian world, 1, 2, 1918, 40-41.

– Days of greater visibility, in: The Friend. A religious, literary, and miscellaneous journal, 58, 36, 1918, 539-540.

– Peace that passes understanding, in: The Friend. A religious, literary, and miscellaneous journal, 58, 47, 1918, 687-688.

– "That which is not brings to naught that which is", in: The Friend. A religious, literary, and miscellaneous journal, 58, 13, 1918, 199-200.

– We have seen his star, in: The Friend. A religious, literary, and miscellaneous journal, 58, 51, 1918, 745-746.

– Where arguments Fail, in: The Friend. A religious, literary, and miscellaneous journal, 58, 16, 1918, 247-248.

– The way of Contagion, in: Friends' Intelligencer, 75, 16, 1918, 250.

– Loyalty and logic, in: London Friend, 75, 43, 1918, 675-676.

– Trying the better Way, in: The Friend. A religious, literary, and miscellaneous journal, 59, 13, 1919, 183-185.

– A long distance call, in: The Friend. A religious, literary, and miscellaneous journal, 59, 44, 1919, 667-668.

– Conquering by an inner force, in: The Friend. A religious, literary, and miscellaneous journal, 59, 40, 1919, 605-606.

– New heaven and a new earth, in: The Friend. A religious, literary, and miscellaneous journal, 59, 37, 1919, 565-567.

– Some new reasons for "Loving enemies", in: The Friend. A religious, literary, and miscellaneous journal, 59, 1919, 29, 1919, 449-450.

– The search for a refuge, in: The Friend. A religious, literary, and miscellaneous journal, 59, 32, 1919, 491-492.

– Trying the better way, in: The World Tomorrow. A journal looking toward a Christian world, 2, 4, 1919, 85-87.

– New heavens and a new earth, in: The World Tomorrow. A journal looking toward a Christian world, 2, 9, 1919, 252-253.

– "The Church of the living God", in: The Friend. A religious, literary, and miscellaneous journal, 59, 49, 1919, 735.

– The new born out of the old, in: The Friend. A religious, literary, and miscellaneous journal, 59, 16, 1919, 229-230.

– Things present and things to come, in: The Friend. A religious, literary, and miscellaneous journal, 59, 26, 1919, 403-404.

– Religion as reality, life and power, Philadelphia 1919 (The William Penn Lectures 1919).

– A religion in life, in: The American Friend, 7, 9, 1919, 197.

– Report of American Commissions of the Conference of All Friends. The fundamental basis of the peace testimony. Being report of commission 1, Philadelphia 1919.

– The world within, in: Friends' Intelligencer, 77, 1, 1920, 1.

– Group-Silence, in: Friends' Intelligencer, 77, 5, 1920, 68.

– Friends and the present hour, in: Friends' Intelligencer, 77, 51, 1920, 801-802.

– Why life involves sacrifice, in: The Quaker. A fortnightly journal devoted to the Religious Society of Friends, 1, 5, 1920, 52-53.

– Where the beyond breaks through, in: The Friend. A religious, literary, and miscellaneous journal, 60, 3, 1920, 25-26.

– Another kind of hero, in: The Friend. A religious, literary, and miscellaneous journal, 60, 18, 1920, 251-252.

– He came to himself, in: The Friend. A religious, literary, and miscellaneous journal, 60, 8, 1920, 101-102.

– The crest rivalries of life, in: The Friend. A religious, literary, and miscellaneous journal, 60, 38, 1920, 589-590.

– Preparation for life's greatest business, in: The Friend. A religious, literary, and miscellaneous journal, 60, 31, 1920, 469-470.

– The nature and authority of conscience, in: The American Friend, 8, 36, 1920, 787.

– Friends and the present hour, in: The American Friend, 8, 51, 1920, 1108.

– The nature and authority of conscience. Swarthmore Lecture, 1920 (2), Central Hill, Westminster, 12th August, in: The Friend. A religious, literary, and miscellaneous journal, 60, 33, 1920, 504-505.

– The better possession, in: The Friend. A religious, literary, and miscellaneous journal, 60, 24, 1920, 363-364.

– Peace that passes understanding, Harrogate, ca. 1920 (Yorkshire 1905 Committee).

– The restatement of the Quaker faith, in: The Friends' Quarterly Examiner. A religious, social and miscellaneous review, 54, 1920, 67-74.

– The religious significance of death, in: The Friends' Quarterly Examiner. A religious, social and miscellaneous review, 54, 1920, 350-361.

– The reinterpretation and restatement of the Quaker faith, in: The Friends' Quarterly Examiner. A religious, social and miscellaneous review, 54, 1920, 67-74.

– The nature and authority of conscience, London 1920 (The Swarthmore Lecture, 13, 1920).

– Why I am a Quaker? Philadelphia, ca. 1920. Philadelphia 1926[2]. Philadelphia 1940[3].

– Preparation for worship, Philadelphia, ca. 1920.

– The later periods of Quakerism, vol. 2, London 1921 (The Quaker History Series, 6).

– A religion of power, Philadelphia 1921 (Pennsbury Leaflet 4).

– The burden of the world. Address of Rufus M. Jones at Meeting in Philadelphia, October 13, 1921, in: The American Friend, 9, 44, 1921, 890.

– A call to Friends everywhere! In: Friends' Intelligencer, 78, 48, 1921, 753-755.

– A call to Friends everywhere! In: The American Friend, 9, 47, 1921, 954.

– A personal message to Friends, in: The American Friend, 9, 2, 1921, 23.

– What the world needs, in: Friends' Intelligencer, 78, 47, 1921, 739.

– What the world needs, in: The American Friend, 9, 8, 1921, 141.

– Silence as a source of power, in: The American Friend, 9, 27, 1921, 536.

– Quakerism of the future. The centennial address, in: The American Friend, 9, 34, 1921, 679-682.

– The great hope, in: The Friend. A religious, literary, and miscellaneous journal, 61, 2, 1921, 17-18.

– Great ones among the lowly, in: The Friend. A religious, literary, and miscellaneous journal, 61, 6, 1921, 81-82.

– In the days of youth, in: The Friend. A religious, literary, and miscellaneous journal, 61, 16, 1921, 243-244.

– The making of a prophet, in: The Friend. A religious, literary, and miscellaneous journal, 61, 19, 1921, 287-289.

– Four boys who became disciples, in: The Friend. A religious, literary, and miscellaneous journal, 61, 29, 1921, 469-471.

– The maiden who came back to life, in: The Friend. A religious, literary, and miscellaneous journal, 61, 34, 1921, 551-553.

– Simon becomes Peter, in: The Friend. A religious, literary, and miscellaneous journal, 61, 39, 1921, 631-633.

– Mary of Magdala, in: The Friend. A religious, literary, and miscellaneous journal, 61, 45, 1921, 745-746.

– What the man of Kerioth dreamed about, in: The Friend. A religious, literary, and miscellaneous journal, 61, 51, 1921, 877-878.

– The leaven of good-will, in: The American Friend, 10, 2, 1922, 21.

– A religion of power, in: The American Friend, 10, 2, 1922, 27.

– A word for the hour, in: The American Friend, 10, 11, 1922, 201.

– What Mary saw, in: The American Friend, 10, 33, 1922, 653-654.

– God waking in the garden in the cool of the day, in: The Friend. A religious, literary, and miscellaneous journal, 63, 4, 1922, 58.

– Preparation for life's greatest business, Philadelphia 1922 (Pennsbury Leaflet 14).

– What the Roman centurion saw, in: The Friend. A religious, literary, and miscellaneous journal, 62, 1, 1922, 6-7.

– The way, in: The Friend. A religious, literary, and miscellaneous journal, 62, 47, 1922, 822.

– The cross-roads once more and some guide-posts, in: The Friend. A religious, literary, and miscellaneous journal, 62, 11, 1922, 181-183.

– The Five Years Meeting, in: The Friend. A religious, literary, and miscellaneous journal, 62, 39, 1922, 660.

– Mary of the ages, in: The Friend. A religious, literary, and miscellaneous journal, 62, 29, 1922, 505-506.

– Religion natural to the human soul, in: The Friend. A religious, literary, and miscellaneous journal, 62, 25, 1922, 441-443.

– The Religious tendency - Whither? In: The Friend. A religious, literary, and miscellaneous journal, 62, 43, 1922, 741-742.

– The cross-roads and some guide boards, in: Christian Century. A journal of religion, 39, 4, 1922, 101-103.

– A word for the hour, in: The Friend. A religious, literary, and miscellaneous journal, 62, 12, 1922, 201-202.

– Das zwiefache Suchen. Über Versöhnung und Gebet, Berlin 1923.

– Thinking over an experience, in: The Friend. A religious, literary, and miscellaneous journal, 63, 2, 1923, 21-22.

– The unused spices, in: The Friend. A religious, literary, and miscellaneous journal, 63, 36, 1923, 689-690.

– If Jesus came to Philadelphia, in: The Friend. A religious, literary, and miscellaneous journal, 63, 25, 1923, 481-484.

– The path breaker, in: The American Friend, 11, 5, 1923, 81.

– A religion of power, in: The American Friend, 11, 8, 1923, 148.

– The more excellent way, in: The American Friend, 11, 32, 1923, 622.

– Prepares to observe Fox tercentenary, in: The American Friend, 11, 45, 1923, 887.

– Tercentenary of the birth of George Fox, in: Friends' Intelligencer, 80, 45, 1923, 763.

– If Jesus came to Philadelphia, in: Friends' Intelligencer, 80, 46, 1923, 772-775.

– A personal message to every Friend, in: Friends' Intelligencer, 80, 51, 1923, 857-858.

– Tercentenary of George Fox, in: The Homiletic Review. An international magazine of religion, theology, and philosophy, 80, 7, 1924, 25.

– The fascination of dualism, in: The Friend. A religious, literary, and miscellaneous journal, 64, 7, 1924, 335-336.

– Another pre-Fox Quaker, in: The Friend. A religious, literary, and miscellaneous journal, 64, 31, 1924, 667-668.

– George Fox's letter to the Governor of Barbadoes, in: The Friend. A religious, literary, and miscellaneous journal, 64, 36, 1924, 759-760.

– The Barbadoes letter again, in: The Friend. A religious, literary, and miscellaneous journal, 64, 43, 1924, 896-897.

– Some contributions of the Quakers to American idealism, in: Canadian journal of religious thought, 1, 10, 1924, 481-490.

– Die Lehre der Quäker. Eine Religion des tätigen Lebens, Berlin 1924.

– The faith of Friends. An excerpt from "The Story of George Fox", Phila-delphia, ca. 1925.

– Overcoming evil - The way of pacifism, in: The World Tomorrow. A jour-nal looking toward a Christian world, 8, 4, 1925, 108-109.

– George Fox, Uppsala 1925.

– Ministry (J. Barnard Walton), in: Friends' Intelligencer, 82, 6, 1925, 104-105.

– The nursery of spiritual life, in: Friends' Intelligencer, 82, 82, 1925, 344.

– Deplores party cries as inadequate, in: The American Friend, 13, 20, 1925, 360.

– Otherism, in: Friends' Intelligencer, 82, 33, 1925, 647.

– Worship as a unifying force, in: Religious Education, 20, 10, 1925, 349-351.

– Why we are here, in: The Farm Journal, 49, 9, 1925, 15.

– Overcoming evil - the way of pacifism, in: World Tomorrow. A journal looking toward a Christian world, 8, 4, 1925, 108-109.

– Quäkerglaube, Leipzig, ca. 1925. Bad Pyrmont 1947[2].

– A key that doth open, in: The Friend. A religious and literary journal, 65, 25, 1925, 29-30.

– The spiritual foundations of character, in: The Friend. A religious and liter-ary journal, 65, 9, 1925, 163-164.

– Overcoming evil - the way of pacifism, in: The Friend. A religious and liter-ary journal, 65, 18, 1925, 351-353.

– Worship as a unifying force, in: The Friend. A religious and literary journal, 65, 42, 1925, 897-899.

– Submerged energies, in: The Friend. A religious and literary journal, 65, 49, 1925, 1053-1054.

– A curious defence of the inner light, in: The Friend. A religious and literary journal, 66, 7, 1926, 126-127.

– A sixth sense, in: The Friend. A religious and literary journal, 66, 18, 1926, 349-350.

– Meditations on a lost day, in: The Friend. A religious and literary journal, 66, 34, 1926, 733-734.

– A retreat on the Taishan, in: The Friend. A religious and literary journal, 66, 42, 1926, 931-932.

– A Chinese prophet who failed, in: The Friend. A religious and literary journal, 66, 48, 1926, 1055-1056.

– The Quaker's faith, Philadelphia 1926. Philadelphia 1943[2].

– Why I am a Quaker. Confessions of faith, 6, in: Forum, 75, 6, 1926, 852-859.

– Some solemn facts, in: Friends' Intelligencer, 83, 19, 1926, 370.

– Some solemn facts, in: The American Friend, 14, 18, 1926, 285-286.

– Another letter from Rufus M. Jones, in: The American Friend, 14, 33, 1926, 540.

– Rufus M. Jones begins busy days in China. Tells of splendid service done in Y.M.C.A. by Rupert Stanley, Earlham graduate, in: The American Friend, 14, 37, 1926, 604.

– Why I am a Quaker? In: Chesterton, Gilbert K.; Slattery, Charles L.; Coffin, Henry Sloane (ed.): Twelve modern Apostles and their creeds, New York 1926, 110-125.

– Great conference in China reported. Letter from Rufus M. Jones gives facts concerning conference of Christian leaders, in: The American Friend, 14, 38, 1926, 620.

– In mountain retreat between the gates. Rufus M. Jones gives a graphic picture of strenuous but happy days in China, in: The American Friend, 14, 40, 1926, 652.

– The infinite treasure, in: The American Friend, 14, 41, 1926, 669.

– Why I am a Quaker? In: Forum, 75, 6, 1926, 852-859.

– My idea of God, in: Woman's Home Companion, 53, 1, 1926, 21.

– The way of love and cooperation. The William Penn Lecture, in: Friends' Intelligencer, 84, 23, 1927, 449-451.

– The indispensables of life, in: Friends' Intelligencer, 84, 50, 1927, 995-997.

– The world-wide opportunity. Substance of an address delivered in Richmond, Indiana, October 22, 1927. Before the Five Years Meeting of the Friends in America, in: The American Friend, 15, 46, 1927, 780-782.

– The nursery of Souls, in: Survey Graphic, 59, 12, 1927, 311-314.

– The faith and practice of the Quakers, London 1927. London 1927[2]. London 1928[3]. London 1930[4]. London 1938[5]. London 1944[6]. London 1949[7]. Reprint Philadelphia 1958. Reprint Philadelphia 1965. Reprint Richmond 1980. Richmond 1986[2]. Richmond 1997[3]. Richmond 2002[4].

– "Mount Sinai in Arabia", in: The Friend. A religious and literary journal, 62, 2, 1927, 29-30.

– Neti-Neti, in: The Friend. A religious and literary journal, 62, 12, 1927, 246-247.

– New light on the "Inner Light", in: The Friend. A religious and literary journal, 62, 23, 1927, 533-534.

– The ocean of life still atop, in: The Friend. A religious and literary journal, 62, 28, 1927, 647-648.

– Why after thee? In: The Friend. A religious and literary journal, 62, 42, 1927, 949-951.

– The indispensables of life, in: The Friend. A religious and literary journal, 62, 44, 1927, 987-988.

– The watch-tower of faith. A contributed editorial, in: The American Friend, 16, 8, 1928, 127-128.

– The path of the peacemakers, in: The Intercollegian, 46, 12, 1928, 69.

– Für unsere Kinder. Das Mädlein, das wieder zum Leben erweckt wurde, in: Der Quäker. Monatshefte der deutschen Freunde, 5, 3, 1928, 65-69.

– Wiara Kwakroen, Warsaw 1928.

– The fine art of living, in: Girard Trust Company. Christmas Carol Singing, n.p., 1928.

– The inner life, in: International Journal of Religious Education, 4, 6, 1928, 8.

– The path of the peacemakers, in: Federal Council Bulletin. A journal of interchurch cooperation, 11, 1, 1928, 13-14.

– Our Christian task, in: The American Friend, 16, 15, 1928, 251.

– Rufus Jones in Boston. This is an excerpt of his speech "The present day religious message for a materialistic age" Given at the final session of the

Friends of New England in Conference at the Old South Meeting House, April 21, 1928, in: The Christian Leader, 31, 18, 1928, 556-557.

– Interior perfection, in: The American Friend, 16, 38, 1928, 671-672.

– A religion of the spirit, in: The American Friend, 16, 47, 1928, 836-837.

– In pa livets stigar, Stockholm 1928.

– The watch-tower of faith, in: The Friend. A religious and literary journal, 68, 9, 1928, 165-167.

– Beauty for ashes, in: The Friend. A religious and literary journal, 68, 27, 1928, 601-602.

– "We look at the things which are not seen", in: The Friend. A religious and literary journal, 68, 34, 1928, 751-752.

– The sense of reality, in: The Friend. A religious and literary journal, 68, 48, 1928, 1065-1067.

– The new quest, New York 1928. New York 1929[2].

– Une religion de l'esprit, in: L'Echo des Amis, 8, 38, 1929, 1-3.

– Une religion de l'esprit, Paris 1929. Paris 1930[2]. Paris 1937[3].

– The power of prayer, in: The Friend. A religious and literary journal, 69, 2, 1929, 25-26.

– It rains where no man is, in: The Friend. A religious and literary journal, 69, 25 1929, 559-560.

– A religious movement or a peculiar people? In: The Friend. A religious and literary journal, 69, 33, 1929, 727-729.

– The way of wonder, in: The Friend. A religious and literary journal, 69, 39, 1929, 853-855.

– That wider fellowship, in: The Friend. A religious and literary journal, 69, 45, 1929, 993-994.

– An appeal to all American Friends, in: Friends' Intelligencer, 86, 14, 1929, 267.

– An appeal to all American Friends, in: The Friend. A religious and literary journal, 102, 40, 1929, 470.

– The way of wonder. A wireless address given in London on September 22nd. Reproduced by permission of the British Broadcasting Corporation, in: The American Friend, 17, 42, 1929, 764-765.

– A wider Quaker fellowship. Rufus M. Jones expresses a concern, in: The American Friend, 17, 45, 1929, 824-825.

– That wider fellowship, in: The American Friend, 17, 48, 1929, 884-885.

– It rains where no man is, in: The Homiletic Review. An international magazine of religion, theology, and philosophy, 98, 8, 1929, 89-90.

– That wider fellowship, in: The World Outlook. A Quaker survey of international life and service, 77, 1, 1930, 1-2.

– Things that remain to be done, in: The Friend. A religious and literary journal, 103, 47, 1930, 553-554.

– "What will a man give in exchange for his life?" In: The American Friend, 18, 37, 1930, 723-724.

– The man who went half way, in: The American Friend, 18, 40, 1930, 783-784.

– The man who went half way, in: The Friend. A religious and literary journal, 104, 12, 1930, 133-134.

– The man who went half way, in: Friends' Intelligencer, 86, 44, 1930, 864-865.

– "Ye have never gone this way before", in: The Friend. A religious and literary journal, 70, 1, 1930, 1-2.

– Things that remain to be done, in: The Friend. A religious and literary journal, 70, 7, 1930, 133-134.

– The life beyond, in: The Friend. A religious and literary journal, 70, 16, 1930, 325-327.

– "What will a man give in exchange for his life"? In: The Friend. A religious and literary journal, 70, 28, 1930, 631-633.

– The man who went half way, in: The Friend. A religious and literary journal, 70, 37, 1930, 813-814.

– In defence of the faith, 13: Silent worship, in: The Spectator, 164, 1930, 222-223.

– The light within man, in: The Friend. A religious and literary journal, 70, 50, 1930, 1149-1151.

– Worship - the central act of religion, in: The American Friend, 19, 31, 1931, 569.

– Founders' day address, in: The Friend. A religious and literary journal, 105, 25, 1931, 291-293.

– The first requisite for a better world, in: Federal Council Bulletin, 14, 10, 1931, 6.

– It was there all the time, in: The Friend. A religious and literary journal, 71, 9, 1931, 177-178.

– Playing the game of life, in: The Friend. A religious and literary journal, 71, 15, 1931, 305-306.

– Two types of confusion, in: The Friend. A religious and literary journal, 71, 38, 1931, 847-848.

Die Vorbereitung zur Andacht, in: Der Quäker. Monatshefte der deutschen Freunde, 8, 4, 1931, 99-104.

– Quakergeloof en Quakerleven, Dan Haag 1931.

– Hebreeuwsche Helden, Uitgevers 1931.

– The Quaker's faith, in: Weber, Julius A. (ed.): Religions and philosophies in the United States, Los Angeles 1931, 152-156.

– A lost birthday, in: The American Friend, 20, 9, 1932, 147.

– The areas of desolation, in: The American Friend, 20, 18, 1932, 315.

– The areas of desolation, in: Friends' Intelligencer, 89, 19, 1932, 369.

– The areas of desolation, in: The Friend. A religious and literary journal, 105, 45, 1932, 529-530.

– The dynamic of William Penn, in: The Friend. A religious and literary journal, 106, 19, 1932, 217-219.

– The dynamic of William Penn, in: Friends' Intelligencer, 89, 47, 1932, 929-930.

– A lost birthday, in: The Friend. A religious and literary journal, 90, 14, 1932, 265-266.

– A Quaker forerunner, in: The Friends' Quarterly Examiner. A religious, social and miscellaneous review, 261, 1, 1932, 47-54.

– Seventy notable years, in: The American Friend, 21, 7, 1933, 79-80.

– Give us the higher want, in: The American Friend, 21, 8, 1933, 91-92.

– A great teacher, in: The Friend. A religious and literary journal, 106, 47, 1933, 553-554.

– The passing of a great teacher, in: The American Friend, 21, 26, 1933, 345.

– Historical address. Delivered from the steps of founders hall, in: The Friend. A religious and literary journal, 108, 8, 1933, 119-120.

– "Make me as one of thy hired servants", in: The Friend. A religious and literary journal, 91, 11, 1933, 209-210.

– "As a man's hand to a man": A testimony, in: The Friend. A religious and literary journal, 91, 17, 1933, 337-338.

– "The oyster man", in: The Friend. A religious and literary journal, 91, 51, 1933, 1153-1154.

– Jezus en zijn Vrienden, Uitgevers 1933.

– Psychical experiences in Quaker Meeting, in: Friends' Intelligencer, 90, 6, 1934, 83-85.

– Some Quaker ideals. Abstract of address given at Friends General Conference, Cape May, in: Friends' Intelligencer, 91, 35, 1934, 551 554.

– With low visibility, in: The American Friend, 22, 19, 1934, 340-341.

– Low visibility, in: The Friend. A religious and literary journal, 108, 7, 1934, 99-100.

– Low visibility, in: Friends' Intelligencer, 91, 38, 1934, 602-603.

– To the American Young Friends Fellowship Conference, in: Friends' Intelligencer, 91, 39, 1934, 615.

– The Quakers and their persecutions, in: The Hebrew Union College Monthly, 21, 4, 1934, 7-9.

– Kvekerismen. En Livs-Religion, n.p., 1934.

– "Psychical experiences of Quaker ministers", in: The Friend. A religious and literary journal, 92, 12, 1934, 245-246.

– The miracle of re-creation, in: The Friend. A religious and literary journal, 92, 16, 1934, 331-332.

– A word for the Quaker of to-day, in: The Friend. A religious and literary journal, 92, 31, 1934, 706-707.

– A dean's religion, in: The Friend. A religious and literary journal, 92, 39, 1934, 873-874.

– The far-flung Quaker service, in: The Friend. A religious and literary journal, 102, 47, 1934, 1075-1076.

– What Christ means, in: Friends' Intelligencer, 92, 50, 1935, 792-793.

– An old Quaker area visited, in: The Friend. A religious and literary journal, 108, 16, 1935, 245.

– An old Quaker area revisited. Rufus Jones writes of historic scenes of friendly interest in southern France, in: The American Friend, 23, 3, 1935, 43.

– An old Quaker area visited, in: Friends' Intelligencer, 92, 10, 1935, 150.

– Digging potatoes, in: Friends' Intelligencer, 92, 40, 1935, 629-630.

– Digging potatoes, in: The American Friend, 23, 19, 1935, 375-376.

– The mind of Christ for today. The substance of the opening address at the Five Years Meeting, October 22, 1935, in: The American Friend, 23, 22, 1935, 439-440.

– Dead apple trees, in: The Friend. A religious and literary journal, 109, 10, 1935, 155-156.

– The fellowship council, in: Canadian Friend, 32, 11, 1935, 7.

– What Christ means, in: The Friend. A religious and literary journal, 93, 1, 1935, 1-2.

– Low visibility, in: The Friend. A religious and literary journal, 93, 23, 1935, 529-530.

– The mind of Christ for to-day, in: The Friend. A religious and literary journal, 93, 47, 1935, 1067-1068.

– The Five Years Meeting. Held at Richmond, Indiana, from October 22 to 28, in: The Friend. A religious and literary journal, 93, 47, 1935, 1071.

– Dead apple trees, in: The Friend. A religious and literary journal, 93, 50, 1935, 1165-1166.

– The Society of Friends and the sacraments, in: The Friends' Quarterly Examiner. A religious, social and miscellaneous Review, 275, 1935, 97-107.

– The Society of Friends and the sacraments, London 1935. London 1939².

– Waiting for the equinox, in: The Quaker Weekly Journal, 94, 10, 1936, 199-200.

– And who is my neighbor? In: The Quaker Weekly Journal, 94, 27, 1936, 621-622.

– An early interpreter of the inner light, in: The Friend. The Quaker weekly journal, 94, 48, 1936, 1097-1098.

– The Society of Friends and the sacraments, in: Friends' Intelligencer, 93, 23, 1936, 363-366.

– Waiting for the equinox, in: The American Friend, 24, 5, 1936, 87.

– Waiting for the equinox, in: Friends' Intelligencer, 93, 9, 1936, 131-132.

– And who is my neighbor? In: The American Friend, 24, 16, 1936, 323-324.

– When the wind comes northwest, in: Friends' Intelligencer, 93, 43, 1936, 709-710.

– For a new power in life, in: The American Friend, 24, 22, 1936, 451.

– One of the first modern interpreters of inward light (Forerunners of Quakerism, 2), in: Friends' Intelligencer, 93, 49, 1936, 817-818.

– An Apostle of the invisible church (Forerunners of Quakerism, 3), in: Friends' Intelligencer, 93, 51, 1936, 848-849.

– An interpretation of Quakerism. London 1936 (Wayfarer Series, 1). Reprint London 1976. Philadelphia 1981.

– Wat zijn Quakers? n.p., ca. 1936.

– Wider Quaker fellowship, Philadelphia 1936.

– Vennernes Samfund og Sakramentene, Stavanger 1936.

– Pathways to the reality of God (in Braille), vol. 2, Los Angeles 1936.

– The testimony of the soul, New York 1936 (This Volume Constitutes the Ayer Lectures for 1936). New York 1937².

– The Quaker's conception of God, in: Laughlin, Sceva Bright (ed.): Beyond dilemmas. Quaker look at life, New York 1937, 29-45.

– A gentle saint from Sicily (Forerunners of Quakerism, 5), in: The Friend. The Quaker weekly journal, 95, 7, 1937, 143.

– The light on the candlestick (Forerunners of Quakerism, 6), in: The Friend. The Quaker weekly journal, 95, 10, 1937, 207-208.

– The smell of the lily (Forerunners of Quakerism, 7), in: The Friend. The Quaker weekly journal, 95, 14, 1937, 296-297.

– The stream comes to England (Forerunners of Quakerism, 8), in: The Friend. The Quaker weekly journal, 95, 16, 1937, 339-340.

– Covenant of grace (Forerunners of Quakerism, 9), in: The Friend. The Quaker weekly journal, 95, 24, 1937, 557-558.

– Sparkles of glory (Forerunners of Quakerism, 10), in: The Friend. The Quaker weekly journal, 95, 29, 1937, 667-668.

– Two sons of thunder and consolation (Forerunners of Quakerism, 6), in: The Friend. The Quaker weekly journal, 95, 1937, 743-744.

– A seeker who became a Quaker finder (Forerunners of Quakerism, 12), in: The Friend. The Quaker weekly journal, 95, 38, 1937, 845-846.

– The basis of Quaker Optimism, in: The Friend. The Quaker weekly journal, 95, 37, 1937, 823-825.

– One whose gentleness made him great (Forerunners of Quakerism, 4), in: Friends' Intelligencer, 94, 3, 1937, 37-38.

– A gentle saint from Sicily in the goodly fellowship (Forerunners of Quakerism, 5), in: Friends' Intelligencer, 94, 9, 1937, 141.

– "The light on the candlestick" (Forerunners of Quakerism, 6), in: Friends' Intelligencer, 94, 14, 1937, 225-226.

– The stream comes to England (Forerunners of Quakerism, 8), in: Friends' Intelligencer, 94, 21, 1937, 353-354.

– The new smell (Forerunners of Quakerism, 7), in: Friends' Intelligencer, 94, 17, 1937, 290-291.

– "Covenant of grace" (Forerunners of Quakerism, 9), in: Friends' Intelligencer, 94, 24, 1937, 400-401.

– A seeker who became a Quaker finder (Forerunners of Quakerism, 10), in: Friends' Intelligencer, 94, 28, 1937, 467-468.

– Sparkles of glory (Forerunners of Quakerism, 11), in: Friends' Intelligencer, 94, 34, 1937, 563-564. – New ways for a new time, in: Friends' Intelligencer, 94, 36, 1937, 595-597.

– The Friends' World Conference, in: The Friend. A religious and literary journal, 111, 7, 1937, 100-101.

– Impressions of the conference, in: Friends' Intelligencer, 94, 39, 1937, 662.

– As viewed by the clerk. Rufus Jones appraises the conference, in: The American Friend, 25, 20, 1937, 409-410.

– The Quaker message, in: The Friend. A religious and literary journal, 111, 8, 1937, 123-124.

– Opening address at Friends World Conference, in: Friends' Intelligencer, 94, 41, 1937, 689-690.

– Over the ocean of darkness. Conference broadcast by Rufus Jones, in: The American Friend, 25, 21, 1937, 432-434.

– Friends and the Far East crisis, in: The Friend. A religious and literary journal, 111, 9, 1937, 157.

– The world is yours. Abstract of addresses given at New York Yearly Meeting, in: Friends' Intelligencer, 94, 25, 1937, 417-418.

– Two sons of thunder and consolation (Forerunners of Quakerism, 12), in: Friends' Intelligencer, 94, 43, 1937, 721-722.

– The inward light, in: Friends World Conference, 1937, n.p., 1937, 23-26 (Report of Commission, 1).

– The spiritual message of the Religious Society of Friends, in: Friends World Conference, 1937, n.p., 1937, 7-16 (Report of Commission, 1).

– Over the ocean of darkness, Philadelphia 1937 (The Woolman Series of Friendly Papers, 8).

– The conference broadcast message, in: Friends World Conference. Official report. Held at Swarthmore and Haverford colleges near Philadelphia, Pennsylvania. September 1st to 8th 1937. Prepared by an editorial committee appointed by the conference business committee, Philadelphia 1937, 11-14.

– World-wide work of the American Friends Service Committee, in: Bulletin of the Friends' Historical Association, 26, 1, 1937, 19-21.

– Die Rundfunkbotschaft der Konferenz, in: Redaktionsausschuß (ed.): Welt-konferenz der Freunde. Autorisierter Bericht. Gehalten in den Colleges zu Swarthmore und Haverford bei Philadelphia, Pennsylvanien, vom 1. bis 9. September 1937, Philadelphia 1937, 11-14.

– Who wrote one of the greatest books ever written? In: The Friends' Quar-terly Examiner. A religious, social and miscellaneous review, 277, 7, 1937, 229-234.

– Quakers at the frontier, in: The Friend. The Quaker weekly journal, 96, 11, 1938, 209-212.

– Imaginary lines, in: The Friend. The Quaker weekly journal, 96, 1938, 748-750.

– Up against the element of "tother", in: The Friend. The Quaker weekly journal, 96, 1938, 767-768.

– Quakers at the frontier, in: Friends' Intelligencer, 95, 95, 1938, 103-107.

– Imaginary lines, in: The American Friend, 26, 16, 1938, 323-324.

– Imaginary lines, in: Friends' Intelligencer, 95, 34, 1938, 563-564.

– Up against the element of "t'other", in: Friends' Intelligencer, 95, 37, 1938, 612-613.

– Up against the element of "tother", in: The American Friend, 26, 19, 1938, 387-388.

– Unsuspected forces in areas of hate, in: Friends' Intelligencer, 95, 52, 1938, 855-856.

– Gedachte Linien, in: Der Quäker. Monatshefte der deutschen Freunde, 15, 10, 1938, 311-312.

– It is time to awake out of sleep, in: The Friend. The Quaker weekly journal, 97, 3, 1939, 41.

– The human faces, in: The Friend. The Quaker weekly journal, 97, 10, 1939, 191-193.

– The philosophy of Quaker service, in: The Friend. The Quaker weekly journal, 97, 24, 1939, 513-515.

– The philosophy of Quaker service (2), in: The Friend. The Quaker weekly journal, 97, 25, 1939, 536-537.

– Dr. Rufus Jones. Chairman, American Friends Service Committee, in: French, Paul Comly (ed.): Common sense neutrality. Mobilizing for peace, New York 1939, 141-142.

– When compulsion cannot compel, in: The American Friend, 27, 3, 1939, 50-51.

– Serenity and adventure, in: Friends' Intelligencer, 96, 16, 1939, 263-264.

– The philosophy of Quaker service, in: Friends' Intelligencer, 96, 24, 1939, 391-394.

– An appeal for tolerance, in: The Friend. A religious and literary journal, 112, 26, 1939, 488.

– For a larger numerator, in: The American Friend, 27, 16, 1939, 320-321.

– Quaker world in Spain, in: The Christian Century. Published weekly, 56, 34, 1939, 1026.

– A brief message to Friends in America, in: The Friend. A religious and literary journal, 112, 6, 1939, 83-84.

– A brief message to Friends in America, in: Friends' Intelligencer, 96, 38, 1939, 615.

– To Friends in America. A brief message, in: The American Friend, 27, 20, 1939, 405.

– On the side of the angles, in: Friends' Intelligencer, 96, 52, 1939, 839-840.

– What can Americans do for humanity today? In: America's Town Meeting of the Air. Town meeting bulletin, 5, 12, 1939, 13-16.

– To Friends in America, in: World Affairs, 102, 12, 1939, 197.

– A way of life and service. A lecture delivered on the Nellie Heldt Lecture Fund, Oberlin 1939 (Nellie Heldt Lectures, 1).

– Vom Menschenantlitz, in: Der Quäker. Monatshefte der deutschen Freunde, 16, 4, 1939, 112-115.

– The philosophy of Quaker service, n.p., 1939. N.p., 1940[2] (American Friends Service Committee, Bulletin 166).

– On the side of the angles, in: London Friend. The Quaker weekly journal, 98, 9, 1940, 123-124.

– "Stand on thy feet", in: London Friend. The Quaker weekly journal, 98, 43, 1940, 591-592.

– Jones, Rufus Matthew; Carver, Washington George; Clark, Glenn; Lester, Muriel: Let us pray, in: The Christian Century. Published weekly, 57, 14, 1940, 445-446.

– Jones, Rufus Matthew; Carver, Washington George; Clark, Glenn; Lester, Muriel: Prayer that prevails, in: The Christian Century. Published weekly, 57, 19, 1940, 603-604.

– Dedicated to a better way. The words with which Rufus M. Jones opened the 1940 session of the Five Years Meeting of Friends, in: The American Friend, 28, 23, 1940, 469.

– The high moment for Quakerism, in: The American Friend, 27, 23, 1940, 472-476.

– The spirit of Christmas, in: Friends' Intelligencer, 97, 51, 1940, 815-816.

– Build anew in your own bosom, in: Canadian Friend, 37, 9, 1940, 5-7.

– Christmas spirit, in: Parents Magazine, 15, 1, 1940, 13.

– Rethinking Quaker principles, Wallingford 1940 (Pendle Hill Pamphlet, 8).

– On the side of the angles, in: Canadian Friend, 36, 5, 1940, 5-6.

– A new year's letter, in: London Friend. The Quaker weekly journal, 99, 6, 1941, 62-63.

– Seeing in the dark, in: London Friend. The Quaker weekly journal, 99, 16, 1941, 187-188.

– The vital cell, in: London Friend. The Quaker weekly journal, 99, 26, 1941, 307-308.

– "Thou must act". Rufus Jones on peace building, in: London Friend. The Quaker weekly journal, 99, 40, 1941, 473-474.

– Unconscious preparation, in: London Friend. The Quaker weekly journal, 99, 45, 1941, 519-520.

– The vital cell, in: Friends' Intelligencer, 98, 14, 1941, 211-212.

– The local meeting - the vital cell. Substance of the William Penn Lecture, Philadelphia Yearly Meeting, March 30, 1941, in: The American Friend, 29, 9, 1941, 171-172.

– The prophetic element in Quakerism, in: Friends' Intelligencer, 98, 31, 1941, 491-492.

– Kingdom building without furlough. From his William Penn Lecture, "The vital cell", in: The American Friend, 29, 17, 1941, 346, 352.

– An appeal to Friends, in: Friends' Intelligencer, 98, 51, 1941, 813.

– The third order, in: Inward Light, 12, 12, 1941, 3-6.

– The vital cell. Delivered at Arch Street Meeting House, Philadelphia, Philadelphia 1941 (William Penn Lecture, 1941). Birmingham 1942[2].

– Sie heilen die Herzen, in: Der Quäker. Monatshefte der deutschen Freunde, 18, 1, 1941, 4-10.

– Die Versöhnung, in: Der Quäker. Monatshefte der deutschen Freunde, 1941, 18, 4, 49-53.

– "Kinder des Lichts", in: Der Quäker. Monatshefte der deutschen Freunde, 18, 6, 1941, 82-86.

– "Lebendig nahe ist er dir!", in: Der Quäker. Monatshefte der deutschen Freunde, 18, 7, 1941, 98-99.

– Our present duty. A message sent to all meetings, in: The Friend. A religious and literary journal, 115, 13, 1941, 210.

– Kvaekernes Tro og Virke, Koebenhavn 1941. Koebenhavn 1953[2].

– Kvaekergeloof en Quakerleven, Koebenhavn 1941.

– Are we ready for a time like this? In: Friends' Intelligencer, 99, 66, 1942, 731-732.

– The bread and water of life, in: The Friend. The Quaker weekly journal, 100, 13, 1942, 97-98.

– Quaker research, in: Friend. A religious and literary journal, 115, 24, 1942, 435-437.

– Quaker research, in: The Friend. A religious and literary journal, 115, 24, 1942, 435-437.

– Thinking back and pressing forward, in: London Friend. The Quaker weekly journal, 100, 1942, 1, 4-5.

– Some Pisgah reflections, in: Friends' Intelligencer, 100, 5, 1943, 67-70.

– Were the Quaker founders consistent peace-makers? In: The Friend. A religious and literary journal, 116, 22, 1943, 346-347.

– Hitherto-henceforth, in: The Friend. The Quaker weekly journal, 101, 1, 1943, 1-2.

– The turning point in the 100 Years, in: The Friend. The Quaker weekly journal, 101, 7, 1943, 110-111.

– Towards the land of promise. Rufus M. Jones' 80th birthday survey, in: The Friend. The Quaker weekly journal, 101, 14, 1943, 229-231.

– Are we ready for a time like this? In: The Friend of Australia and New Zealand. A religious, literary, and miscellaneous journal, August 19, 1943, 1-2.

– "Woe is me for I dwell in Meshech", in: Friends' Intelligencer, 100, 41, 1943, 663-664.

– A call for renewed life. A speech, in: The American Friend, 31, 10, 1943, 194-195.

– Province of Quaker periodicals, in: Friends' Intelligencer, 100, 50, 1943, 818-819.

– On broken pieces, in: The Friend. The Quaker weekly journal, 101, 51, 1943, 841-842.

– The stirrings in America, in: The Atlantic Monthly, 172, 6, 1943, 99-101.

– Kväkarnas Tro och Livsaskadning, Stockholm 1943. Skelleftea 1997².

– The new holy family, in: The American Friend, 31, 5, 1943, 87-88.

– A call for renewed life. A speech, in: The American Friend, 31, 10, 1943, 194-195.

– The birth of the American Friend, in: The American Friend, 32, 14, 1944, 267-268.

– Reflections of an "ancient" Friend, in: Friends' Intelligencer, 101, 2, 1944, 20-21.

– Are we ready? In: Friends' Intelligencer, 101, 11, 1944, 163-164.

– The winnowing fan, in: The Friend. The Quaker weekly journal, 102, 16, 1944, 241-242.

– The basis of unity, in: Friends' Intelligencer, 101, 26, 1944, 407-408.

– The heart of the Quaker faith. Delivered at Upper Dublin Meeting House, Ambler 1944 (Rufus M. Jones Lecture, 1).

– Are we ready? Philadelphia 1944.

– What will get us ready? In: Friends' Intelligencer, 102, 4, 1945, 51-53.

– Ministry for the whole man, in: Friends' Intelligencer, 102, 23, 1945, 363-365.

– The Quaker conception of man, in: Friends' Intelligencer, 102, 37, 1945, 587-589.

– The Friends of God, in: The Friend. A religious and literary journal, 118, 16, 1945, 245-246.

– Claim everything, Philadelphia, ca. 1945 (The Woolman Series of Friendly Papers, 18).

– Original Quakerism a movement, not a sect. Given before the Five Years Meeting of Friends in America in session, October 18, 1945, at Richmond, Indiana, n.p., 1945 (The Isaac T. and Lida K. Johnson Lecture, 1945).

– What will get us ready? In: Friends' Intelligencer, 102, 4, 1945, 51-53.

– The spiritual house, in: The Friend. The Quaker weekly journal, 103, 31, 1945, 505-506.

– A movement - not a sect, in: The Friend. The Quaker weekly journal, 103, 46, 1945, 769-771.

– Ministry for the whole man, in: Friends' Intelligencer, 102, 23, 1945, 363-365.

– Ein Gefühl für das, was lebendig ist, in: Der Quäker. Monatshefte der deutschen Freunde, 20, 5/6, 1946, 85-86.

– Die Fackelträger. Ein Veteran ruft die neue Generation der Freunde, in: Der Quäker. Monatshefte der deutschen Freunde, 20, 5/6, 1946, 70-73.

– Eine Darlegung des Quäkertums, Bad Pyrmont 1946.

– La fe y la experiencia de los Cuáqueros, Buenos Aires 1946.

– The Quaker conception of man, in: Friends' Intelligencer, 103, 2, 1946, 19-20.

– We must get ready to go forward, in: Jones, Rufus (ed.): Together. New York 1946, 12-23.

– Malice toward none, charity for all, in: Friends' Intelligencer, 103, 3, 1946, 40-41.

– What is "plain language" and why? In: Friends' Intelligencer, 103, 13, 1946, 200-201.

– The wider Quaker fellowship, in: Friends' Intelligencer, 103, 31, 1946, 461-462.

– The great succession of torch bearers, in: Friends' Intelligencer, 103, 46, 1946, 647-651.

– The great succession of torch bearers. A lecture delivered at Arch Street Meeting House, Philadelphia, Nov. 3, 1946, Philadelphia 1946.

– Malice toward none, charity for all, in: The Friend. A religious and literary journal, 119, 14, 1946, 211-212.

– Eine Bewegung - nicht eine Sekte, in: Mitteilungen der Religiösen Gesellschaft der Freunde (Quäker), 1946, 20, 3, 1-2.

– When the earthquake comes, in: The Friend. The Quaker weekly journal, 104, 23, 1946, 453-454.

– The four highways of the school, in: The Friend. The Quaker weekly journal, 104, 37, 1946, 725-726.

– Kvekernes Tro og Virke, Stavanger 1947.

– The torch bearers. A veteran's call to the new generation of Friends, in: The Friend. The Quaker weekly journal, 105, 1, 1947, 1-3.

– An instinct for what is vital, in: The Friend. The Quaker weekly journal, 105, 4, 1947, 65.

– The hand of a man, in: The Friend. The Quaker weekly journal, 105, 42, 1947, 838-839.

– "They had the hands of a man under the wings", in: Friends' Intelligencer, 104, 40, 1947, 534.

– What the modern man can believe, n.p., 1947.

– A Friend's tribute, in: Rowntree, John Wilhelm: Claim your inheritance. Essays on man's relation to God, London 1948, 12-14.

– The date to commemorate, in: Friends' Intelligencer, 105, 16, 1948, 219-220.

– A call to a new installment of heroic spirit, in: Friends' Intelligencer, 105, 29, 1948, 407-409.

– Religion as a dynamic, in: Friends' Intelligencer, 105, 41, 1948, 575.

– A call to a new installment of heroic spirit, in: The Friend. A religious and literary journal, 122, 2, 1948, 19-22.

– The American Friends Service Committee, in: Phillips, Dorothy Berkley (ed.): The choice is always ours. An anthology on the religious way, chosen from psychological, religious, philosophical and biographical sources, New York 1948, 447-449.

– God in Christ, in: The Friend. The Quaker weekly journal, 106, 25, 1948, 497-498.

– The time has come. Enlarge our borders! Special to the American Friend, in: The American Friend, 55, 14, 1948, 220-221.

– The third order as a "vital cell", in: Phillips, Dorothy Berkley (ed.): The choice is always ours. An anthology on the religious way, chosen from psychological, religious, philosophical and biographical sources, New York 1948, 457-459. Reprint Wheaton 1975.

– God as revealed in Jesus Christ, in: Phillips, Dorothy Berkley (ed.): The choice is always ours. An anthology on the religious way, chosen from psychological, religious, philosophical and biographical sources, New York 1948, 487-489. Reprint Wheaton 1975.

– A call to what is vital, New York 1948. New York 1949[2]. New York 1950[3].

– The assurance of sight, in: The Friend. The Quaker weekly journal, 106, 15, 1948, 289-290.

– Das Tagebuch des Cyrus Pringle, in: Der Quäker. Monatsschrift der deutschen Freunde, 24, 1/2, 1949, 7-21.

– God in Christ, in: The Friend. A religious and literary journal, 122, 4, 1948, 50.

– Ministry for the whole man. Reprinted by Friends central bureau by permission of Friends' Intelligencer, Philadelphia, ca. 1950.

– Rethinking Quaker principles, in: Maurer, Herrymon (ed.): The Pendle Hill reader. New York (1950), 161-183.

– Rufus Jones speaks. Edited by Leonard S. Kenworthy, n.p., 1951.

– Fosdick, Harry Emerson (ed.): Rufus Jones speaks to our time. An anthology, New York 1951. London 1953[2]. New York 1961[3].

– Aussprüche, in: Der Quäker. Monatsschrift der deutschen Freunde, 24, 8, 1952, 124.

– Das Reich Gottes im Menschen. Eine Betrachtung über die Ansichten der ersten Freunde und der Versuch einer modernen Darlegung, in: Der Quäker. Monatshefte der deutschen Freunde, 34, 6, 1960, 87-96.

– Quakerism. A spiritual movement. Six essays. With a sketch of his life by Mary Hoxie Jones, Philadelphia 1963.

– Thou dost open up my life. Selections from the Rufus Jones collection. Edited by Mary Hoxie Jones, Wallingford 1963 (Pendle Hill Pamphlet, 127).

– Cadbury, Henry Joel: Rufus Jones Centennial, 1863-1963, Richmond 1963.

– A Rufus Jones sampler, in: Friends Journal, 9, 2, 1963, 27-28, 35-36.

– Warum wir leben. Köpfe des Weltquäkertums: Rufus M. Jones (1863-1948), in: Der Quäker. Monatsschrift der deutschen Freunde, 45, 9, 1971, 195-196.

– The supreme revelation, in: The Carey Memorial Lectures. Delivered at the annual sessions of Baltimore Yearly Meeting, 2, 1972, 3-12.

– Rufus Jones speaks, in: Kenworthy, Leonard S. (ed.): Sixteen Quaker leaders speak, Richmond 1979, 57-64.

– Selections from the writing of Rufus Jones, in: Steere, Douglas V. (ed.): Quaker spirituality. Selected writings, New York 1984, 261-286. New York 2005.

– Kenworthy, Leonard S. (ed.): Think on these things. An anthology of inspirational quotations, Grand Rapids 1987.

– Oneness and otherness, in: Cell, Edward (ed.): Daily readings from Quaker spirituality, Springfield 1987, 46.

– Social programs and more, in: Cell, Edward (ed.): Daily readings from Quaker spirituality. Springfield 1987, 47.

– Two paths in morality, in: Cell, Edward (ed.): Daily readings from Quaker spirituality, Springfield 1987, 48.

– Blessedness, in: Cell, Edward (ed.): Daily readings from Quaker spirituality, Springfield 1987, 49.

– Personal contagion, in: Cell, Edward (ed.): Daily readings from Quaker spirituality, Springfield 1987, 50.

– Blessed are they who mourn, in: Cell, Edward (ed.): Daily readings from Quaker spirituality, Springfield 1987, 51.

– On being utterly absorbed, in: Cell, Edward (ed.): Daily readings from Quaker spirituality, Springfield 1987, 52.

– A new level of experience, in: Cell, Edward (ed.): Daily readings from Quaker spirituality, Springfield 1987, 53.

– God our refuge, in: Cell, Edward (ed.): Daily readings from Quaker spirituality, Springfield 1987, 54.

– Pacifism, in: Cell, Edward (ed.): Daily readings from Quaker spirituality, Springfield 1987, 56.

– A gathered silence, in: Cell, Edward (ed.): Daily readings from Quaker spirituality, Springfield 1987, 57.

– The practice of human brotherhood, in: Cell, Edward (ed.): Daily readings from Quaker spirituality, Springfield 1987, 58.

– The utterance of persons who were plain, in: West, Jessamy (ed.): The Quaker reader, Wallingford 1992, 202-206.

– "...A unique laboratory experiment which worked", in: West, Jessamy (ed.): The Quaker reader, Wallingford 1992, 416-424.

– The sense of the meeting, in: West, Jessamy (ed.): The Quaker reader, Wallingford 1992, 424-428.

– I go to Philadelphia, in: West, Jessamy (ed.): The Quaker reader, Wallingford 1992, 428-430.

– To those who would like to have closer fellowship with Friends. A letter from Rufus Jones. Edited by the AFSC, Philadelphia, ca. 2000.

– A Rufus Jones companion. Edited by the Wellesley Monthly Meeting of the Religious Society of Friends, Wellesley 2001.

– Essential writings. Edited by Kerry Walters, New York 2001.

Editorials, Introductions, and Forewords

– Editorial letter, in: The American Friend, 10, 34, 1903, 563
– An editorial letter, in: The American Friend, 11, 27, 1904, 443-444.
– Editorial letter. In Kansas, in: The American Friend, 14, 7, 1907, 99-100;
– Editorial letter, in: The American Friend, 14, 43, 1907, 679.
– Editorial letter, in: The American Friend, 16, 26, 1909, 403-404.
– Editorial letter, in: The American Friend, 17, 36, 1910, 567-568.
– Editorial letter, in: The American Friend, 17, 37, 1910, 583.
– Editorial letter, in: The American Friend, 17, 40, 1910, 631.
– Editorial letter, in: The American Friend, 19, 52, 1912, 883-884.
– Introduction, in: Braithwaite, William: The beginnings of Quakerism, London 1912, xxv-xliv. London 1923[2]. Reprint Cambridge 1955. Cambridge 1961[2]. Reprint York 1981.
– Foreword, in: Braithwaite, William; Hodgkin, Henry: The message and mission of Quakerism, London, ca. 1915, 3-4.
– Introduction, in: Rowntree, John William: Man's relation to God and other addresses, London 1917, 3-5 (Pennsbury Series of Modern Quaker Books, 3).
– Introduction, in: Pringle, Cyrus: The record of a Quaker conscience. Cyrus Pringle's diary, New York 1918, 5-19.
– Introduction, in: Braithwaite, William: The second period of Quakerism, London 1919, xxiii-xlvi. London 1921[2] (Quaker History Series, 5).
– Introduction, in: Kelsey, Rayner Wickersham: Centennial history of Moses Brown School, 1819-1919, Providence 1919, xiii-xviii.
– Introduction, in: Emmott, Elizabeth Braithwaite: A short history of Quakerism (Earlier Periods), New York 1923, 17-20.
– Introduction, in: Hirst, Margaret: The Quakers in peace and war. An account of heir peace principles and practice, London 1923, 9-10. Reprint New York 1972.
– Introduction, in: The journal of George Fox, London 1924, ix-xiii. London 1940[2]. Reprint London 1948. Reprint London 1949. Reprint London 1962. Reprint London 1963. Reprint Richmond 1983.

– Preface, in: Fox, George: The short journal and itinerary journals of George Fox. In commemoration of the tercentenary of his birth (1624-1924). Now first published for Friends' Historical Association, Philadelphia, Pennsylvania. Edited by Norman Penney, Cambridge 1925, v.

– Epilogue, in: Fry, A. Ruth: A Quaker adventure. The story of nine years' relief and reconstruction, London 1926, 354-356. Reprint London 1927.

– Foreword, in: Kagawa, Toyohiko: Love. The law of life, Chicago 1929. Reprint London 1930. London 1934[2], vii-viii.

– Introduction, in: Jones, Lester Martin: Quakers in action. Recent humanitarian and reform activities of the American Quakers, New York 1929, xi-xv.

– Foreword, in: Brockbank, Elisabeth: Richard Hubberthorne of Yealand. Yeoman - soldier - Quaker, 1628-1662, London 1929, 13-15.

– Foreword, in: Hodgkin, Henry Theodore: Personality and progress. Garden City 1929, 11-14.

– Introduction, in: Brinton, Howard Haines: The mystic will. Based on a study of the philosophy of Jacob Boehme, New York 1930, ix-xiii.

– Greeting, in: Directory and handbook of Northeast Harbor, Maine 1930, 3.

– Preface, in: Bennett, Charles Andrew Armstrong: A philosophical study of mysticism. An essay. Reprint New Haven 1931, ix-xiii.

– Introduction, in: Wright, Luella: The literary life of the early Friends. 1650-1725. Dissertation New York 1932, xiii-xiv. New York 1966.

– Foreword, in: Hocking, Ernest; Woodward, Frederic; Barbour, Clarence; Betts, Edgar; Brown, Arlo; Emerson, Charles; Houghton, Henry S.; Jones, Rufus Matthew; Merrill, William P.; Scott, Albert L.; Sibley, Harper; Taylor, Henry C.; Woodsmall, Ruth F. (ed.): Re-thinking missions. A laymen's inquiry after one hundred years, New York 1932, ix-xv.

– Foreword, in: Iwahashi, Takeo: Light from darkness, Philadelphia 1932, 5-6.

– Foreword, in: Fort, Adèle Brooks: Splendor in the night. Recording a glimpse of reality. By a pilgrim, Portland 1933, xi-xiv. Portland 1934[3].

– Nachwort, in: Fry, Ruth: Ein Quäker-Wagnis. Die abenteuerliche Geschichte eines Friedensfeldzuges in und nach dem Weltkriege, Nürnberg 1933, 363-364.

– Introduction, in: Gregg, Richard Bartlett: The power of non-violence, Philadelphia 1934, 7-10. Reprint London 1935. New York 1944[2]. Ahmedabad 1949[3]. New York 1951[4].

– Foreword, in: Heath, Effie Margaret: The story of Lucy Stone: Pioneer, London 1935, 11-12.

– Introduction, in: Fox, George: Journal de George Fox, 1624-1690. Fondateur de la Société des amis (Quakers). Récit historique de sa vie, de ses voyages, de ses souffrances et de ses expériences chrétiennes, Paris 1935, xix-xxiii. Paris 1962[2].

– Foreword, in: Cadbury, William Worder; Jones, Mary Hoxie: At the point of a lancet. One hundred years of the Canton Hospital, Shanghai 1935, xi. Shanghai 1936[2].

– Foreword, in: Gilbreath, Joseph Earl: The vision of God and the social order, New York 1936, 7-8.

– Introduction, in: MacIntosh, Margaret Taylor: Joseph Wright Taylor, Founder of Bryn Mawr College, Haverford 1936, xiii-xviii.

– Foreword, in: Hess, Mary Whitcomb (ed.): The name is living. The life and teachings of Isaac Penington, Chicago 1936, 1-4.

– Foreword, in: Jones, Mary Hoxie: Swords into ploughshares. An account of the American Friends Service Committee, 1917-1937, New York 1937, vii-x.

– Foreword, in: Chace, Elizabeth Buffum: Two Quakers sisters. From the original diaries of Elizabeth Buffum Chace and Lucy Buffum Lovell, New York 1937, xiii-xv.

– Introduction, in: Roberts, Richard: The contemporary Christ, New York 1938, v-viii.

– Foreword, in: Moon, Robert Barclay: Stories of the prophets as told to their Friends, Nashville, ca. 1938, 7-10.

– Introduction, in: Stamp, Lord: Christianity and economics, London 1939, v-viii.

– Introduction, in: Hopwood, Percy George Samuel: A testament of faith, New York 1939, vii-x (Great Issues of Life Series).

– Dedication, in: The senior class of Drexel Institute of Technology, 1940
(ed.): The Lexerd. 1940, Philadelphia 1940, 9.

– Introduction, in: Robinson, H. Wheeler: Suffering, human and divine, New
York 1939. Reprint London 1940, 11-14.

– Introduction, in: King, Rachel Hadley: George Fox and the light within,
1650-1660. Dissertation Philadelphia 1940, 5-7.

– Foreword, in: Jackson, Harrison: Two wonderful experiences, London
1940, 1. London 1940². London 1940³.

– Foreword, in: Curtis, Anna: Stories of the underground railroad, New York
1941, v-vii.

– Preface, in: Vernier, Philippe: With the master. A book of mediations, New
York 1943², 5-6.

– Foreword to the American edition, in: Champion, Selwyn Gurney (ed.): The
eleven religions and their proverbial lore. A comparative study, New York
1945, v-vi.

– Foreword, in: Dudley, James: The life of Edward Grubb, 1854-1939. A spiritual pilgrimage, London 1946, 9-10.

– Introduction, in: Jones, Rufus Matthew; Laubach, Frank; Moseley, Rufus;
Jones, Stanley; Clark, Glenn; Judd, Walter; Magee, John; Shoemaker, Samuel
M.; Starr, Dailey; Vereide, Abraham; Harding, Glenn; Thurman, Howard: To-
gether, New York 1946, 7-11.

– Introduction, in: Hinshaw, David: An experiment in friendship, New York
1947, ix-xi.

– Introduction, in: Moore, Emily E.: Travelling with Thomas Story. The life
and travels of an eighteenth-century Quaker, Hertfordshire 1947, xix-xxi.

– Foreword, in: Boehme, Jacob: The way to Christ. In a new translation.
Edited by John Joseph Stoudt, New York 1947, vii-ix.

– Foreword, in: Fox, George: George Fox's "Book of Miracles". Edited by
Henry Cadbury, Cambridge 1948, ix-xiv. New York 1973. Philadelphia 2000².

– Introduction to the American edition, in: Gollancz, Victor: Our threatened
values, Hinsdale 1948, 7-8.

Entries in Dictionaries

– Deliberation, in: Encyclopedia of Religion and Ethics, 4, ca. 1914, 544.

– Flagellants, in: Encyclopedia of Religion and Ethics, 6, 1914, 49-51.

– Ranters, in: Encyclopedia of Religion and Ethics, 10, 1919, 578-580.

– Seekers, in: Encyclopedia of Religion and Ethics, 11, 1921, 350-351.

– Silence, in: Encyclopedia of Religion and Ethics, 11, 1921, 512-513.

– Theurgy, in: Encyclopedia of Religion and Ethics, 12, 1922, 319-320.

– Mysticism (Introductory), in: Encyclopedia of Religion and Ethics, 9, 1925, 83-84.

– Mysticism (Christian, New Testament), in: Encyclopedia of Religion and Ethics, 9, 1925, 89-90.

– Mysticism (Christian, Protestant), in: Encyclopedia of Religion and Ethics, 9, 1925, 101-103;

– Oversoul, in: Encyclopedia of Religion and Ethics, 9, 1925, 584-585.

– Peculiar people, in: Encyclopedia of Religion and Ethics, 9, 1925, 701-703.

– Coffin, Charles Fisher, in: Dictionary of American Biography, 4, 1930, 266.

– Comstock, Elizabeth L., in: Dictionary of American Biography, 4, 1930, 331-332.

– Gibbons, Abigail Hopper, in: Dictionary of American Biography, 7, 1931, 237-238.

– Hicks, Elias, in: Dictionary of American Biography, 9, 1932, 6-7.

– Hoag, Joseph, in: Dictionary of American Biography, 9, 1932, 85-86.

– Hopper, Isaac Tatem, in: Dictionary of American Biography, 9, 1932, 224.

– Hunt, Nathan, in: Dictionary of American Biography, 9, 1932, 389.

– Jay, Allen, in: Dictionary of American Biography, 10, 1933, 3-4.

– Keith, George, in: Dictionary of American Biography, 10, 1933, 289-290.

– Owen, Griffith, in: Dictionary of American Biography, 14, 1934, 118.

– Sands, David, in: Dictionary of American Biography, 16, 1935, 342-343.

– Scattergood, Thomas, in: Dictionary of American Biography, 16, 1935, 410-411.

– Smith, Hannah Withall, in: Dictionary of American Biography, 17, 1935, 274-275.

– Thomas, Richard Henry, in: Dictionary of American Biography, 18, 1936, 443-444.

– Updegraff, David Brainerd, in: Dictionary of American Biography, 19, 1936, 120.

– Waln, Nicholas, in: Dictionary of American Biography, 19, 1936, 386-387.

– Wilbur, John, in: Dictionary of American Biography, 20, 1936, 200.

– Wood, James, in: Dictionary of American Biography, 20, 1936, 460-461.

– Recovering the foundations, in: Stuber, Stanley I.; Clark, Thomas Curtis (ed.): Treasury of the Christian faith. An encyclopedic handbook of the range and witness of Christianity, New York 1949, 83.

– The basic question, in: Stuber, Stanley I.; Clark, Thomas Curtis (ed.): Treasury of the Christian faith. An encyclopedic handbook of the range and witness of Christianity, New York 1949, 83-84.

– A great pilot, in: Stuber, Stanley I.; Clark, Thomas Curtis (ed.): Treasury of the Christian faith. An encyclopedic handbook of the range and witness of Christianity, New York 1949, 88.

– Tribute to a mother, in: Stuber, Stanley I.; Clark, Thomas Curtis (ed.): Treasury of the Christian faith. An encyclopedic handbook of the range and witness of Christianity, New York 1949, 148-149.

– Minimum faith, in: Stuber, Stanley I.; Clark, Thomas Curtis (ed.): Treasury of the Christian faith. An encyclopedic handbook of the range and witness of Christianity, New York 1949, 277.

– Immortal creative literature, in: Stuber, Stanley I.; Clark, Thomas Curtis (ed.): Treasury of the Christian faith. An encyclopedic handbook of the range and witness of Christianity, New York 1949, 33.

– Breaking the microscope, in: Stuber, Stanley I.; Clark, Thomas Curtis (ed.): Treasury of the Christian faith. An encyclopedic handbook of the range and witness of Christianity, New York 1949, 323.

– What counts most, in: Stuber, Stanley I.; Clark, Thomas Curtis (ed.): Treasury of the Christian faith. An encyclopedic handbook of the range and witness of Christianity, New York 1949, 412.

– Arriving where God is, in: Stuber, Stanley I.; Clark, Thomas Curtis (ed.): Treasury of the Christian faith. An encyclopedic handbook of the range and witness of Christianity, New York 1949, 413-414.

– What "eternal" means, in: Stuber, Stanley I.; Clark, Thomas Curtis (ed.): Treasury of the Christian faith. An encyclopedic handbook of the range and witness of Christianity, New York 1949, 429.

– Mysticism, in: Runes, Dagobert (ed.): The Dictionary of Philosophy, New York 1951, 203.

– Spiritualism, in: Runes, Dagobert (ed.): The Dictionary of Philosophy, New York 1951, 300.

ش Part Four

Secondary Sources

IV. SECONDARY SOURCES

Bibliography

– Children of light. In honor of Rufus M. Jones. Edited by Howard H. Brinton, New York 1938, 406-411.

– Rush, Nixon Orwin: A bibliography of the published writings of Rufus Jones, Waterville 1944 (Colby College Monograph, 12).

– T., D. E.: The real monument of Rufus Jones, in: The Friend. A religious and literary journal, 122, 26, 1948, 22-23.

– Rufus Jones speaks to our time. An anthology. Edited by Harry Emerson Fosdick, New York 1951, 287-289.

– Hinshaw, David: Rufus Jones: Master Quaker. A biography, New York 1951, 295-298.

– Vining, Elizabeth Gray: Friend of life, Philadelphia 1958. London 1959[2], 333-334.

– Quakerism. A spiritual movement. Six essays. With a sketch of his life by Mary Hoxie Jones, Philadelphia 1963, 207-208.

– Turner, Angela: A bibliography of Quaker Literature, 1893-1967, Ann Arbor 1973.

– Dunn, Frances Mary: The Quaker collection of the Morris Miller Library, University of Tasmania. A preliminary checklist, n.p., 1973, 39.

– Brodie, Audrey: Books in Society of Friends libraries, Wellington 1996, 79-83 (About Quakers and Quakerism. A Listing of Books in New Zealand Libraries, 1).

– Claus Bernet: Jones, Rufus (1863-1948), in: Biographisch-Bibliographisches Kirchenlexikon, 22, 2003, 633-694.

Literature on Rufus Jones

– Rufus M. Jones on the need of the century, in: The Friend. A religious, literary, and miscellaneous journal, 42, 38, 1902, 606-607.

– Impressions of the summer school, Woodbrooke, in: The Friend. A religious, literary, and miscellaneous journal, 43, 31, 1903, 506-510.

– Farewell to Rufus Jones, in: The Friend. A religious, literary, and miscellaneous journal, 48, 34, 1908, 553-555.

– Brayshaw, A. Neave: The Quakers. Their story and message. London 1921.
London 1927[2]. London 1938[3]. London 1946[4]. London 1953[5]. Reprint London 1969.

– Gittins, Robert: Rufus Jones's visit to Friends' Indian Mission, C. P, in: The
Friend. A religious and literary journal, 62, 3, 1927, 57-58.

– American Friends' Service, in: The Friend. A religious and literary journal,
68, 42, 1928, 940.

– N., G.: Many happy returns! Rufus M. Jones' 70th birthday, in: The Friend.
A religious and literary journal, 91, 3, 1933, 48-50.

– Hughes, Mary: Honouring Rufus M. Jones, in: The Friend. A religious and
literary journal, 91, 6, 1933, 110.

– Regen, Rosalie: Rufus Jones and the Gestapo. Richmond, ca. 1935.

– Children of Light. In honor of Rufus M. Jones. Edited by Howard H. Brinton, New York 1938.

– Cadbury, Henry: "Salute Rufus...": A 75th birthday tribute, in: The Friend.
The Quaker weekly journal, 96, 3, 1938, 45-46.

– Carver, George Washington: Glenn Clark, Rufus Jones, and Muriel Lester.
Prayer that prevails, in: Christian Century. Published weekly, 57, 19, 1940,
603-604.

– Rush, Nixon Orwin: Jones, Rufus M.(atthew), in: Current Biography. Who's
news and why, 7, 10, 1941. Reprint 1969. Reprint 1971, 446-447.

– Herbert Hoover an Rufus M. Jones, den 17. November 1919, in: Buchinger,
Hans (ed.): Quaker German, Pendle Hill 1943, 89-90.

– Harvey, T. Edmund: Commentary. Greetings to Rufus Jones at 80, in: The Friend. The Quaker weekly journal, 101, 4, 1943, 51.

– Brodhead, Charles David: Quaker seer urges spiritual recovery. Rufus M. Jones passes eightieth year - League for Protestant Action says this is righteous war (Correspondence from Philadelphia), in: Christian Century. Published weekly, 60, 7, 1943, 206.

– Rediger, Milo Albert: An interpretation of the philosophy of Rufus Jones with special reference to education. Dissertation New York 1946.

– Theodore Dreiser to Rufus M. Jones, in: Bulletin of Friends' Historical Association, 35, 2, 1946, 62.

– Relax with Rufus. Stories for the holiday week-end, in: The Friend. The Quaker weekly journal, 104, 16, 1946, 309-310.

– Waln, Nora: First-Day with Rufus Jones, in: The Atlantic, 179, 6, 1947, 51-57.

– Comfort, William Wistar: Rufus M. Jones. 1863-1948, in: The Friend. A religious and literary journal 122, 1, 1948, 2-3.

– Watchman: Rufus Jones 85!, in: The Friend. The Quaker weekly journal, 106, 4, 1948, 62-63.

– E., E. T.: Rufus Matthew Jones. Christian mystic and plain Quaker, in: The American Friend, 55, 14, 1948, 219.

– To Rufus Jones - In grateful tribute. From his contemporaries, in: The American Friend, 55, 14, 1948, 221-222.

– Pickett, Clarence: In heroic enterprises, in: The American Friend, 55, 14, 1948, 223-225.

– Trueblood, Elton D.: Rufus Jones as a thinker, in: The American Friend, 55, 14, 1948, 224.

– Cadbury, Henry J.: Contributions to a philosophy, in: The American Friend, 55, 14, 1948, 225.

– Rowntree, John Wilhelm: A Five Years Meeting Friend, in: The American Friend, 55, 14, 1948, 226.

– A life in review. From the American Friends Service Committee, in: The American Friend, 55, 14, 1948, 227.

– Rufus M. Jones. 1863-1948. The story of an integrated life, in: The Friend. The Quaker weekly journal, 106, 26, 1948, 517-522.

– Watchman: The heroic spirit, in: The Friend. The Quaker weekly journal, 106, 31, 1948, 626-627.

– Rufus M. Jones, 1863-1948. Die Geschichte eines vollendeten Lebens, in: Der Quäker. Monatshefte der deutschen Freunde, 22, 3/4, 1948, 227-234.

– Ueda, Tatsunosuke: Quaker scholarship. A few thoughts in memory of Rufus M. Jones, in: The Friend. A religious and literary journal, 122, 4, 1948, 101-103.

– Drake, Thomas E.: Rufus M. Jones, in: Bulletin of Friends' Historical Association, 37, 2, 1948, 84.

– Comfort, William Wistar: Quakers in the modern world, New York 1949.

– Haverford College (ed.): Rufus M. Jones. January 25, 1863 - June 16, 1948. In memoriam, Haverford 1950.

– Hibbert, Gerald: "Christian mystic and plain Quaker", in: The Friend. The Quaker Weekly, 109, 16, 1951, 331-332.

– Hinshaw, David: Rufus Jones: Master Quaker. A biography, New York 1951.

– Krusé, Cornelius: Rufus M. Jones und sein Werk, Bad Pyrmont 1952 (Richard Cary Vorlesung 1952).

– Rufus Jones, in: Der Quäker. Monatsschrift der deutschen Freunde, 24, 8, 1952, 123.

– Dwyer, Eddie L.: The principle of authority in the theology of Rufus Jones. Dissertation Southwestern Baptist Theological Seminary 1952.

– Jacob, Caroline Nicholson: Rufus M. Jones, 1863-1948, in: Jacob, Caroline Nicholson: Builders of the Quaker road, 1652-1952, Chicago 1953, 203-213.

– Whitney, Janet: Rufus Jones. Friend, in: The Atlantic, 193, 1954, 29-33.

– Alsobrook, William Aubrey: The mysticism of Rufus M. Jones. Dissertation Drew University 1954.

– Vipont, Elfrida: The story of Quakerism through three centuries, London 1954. Reprint London 1955. London 1960[2].

– Jones, Mary Hoxie: Rufus M. Jones, London 1955. London 1970² (Quaker Biographies).

– Cooper, Wilmer A.: Rufus M. Jones and the contemporary Quaker view of man. Dissertation Vanderbilt 1956.

– Friedrich, Gerhard: The Dreiser - Jones correspondence, in: Bulletin of Friends' Historical Association, 46, 1, 1957, 23-34.

– Introduction, in: Hazelton, Robert Morton: Let freedom ring! A biography of Moses Brown, New York 1957, xvii-xx.

– Vining, Elizabeth Gray: Friend of life, Philadelphia 1958. London 1959².

– Vining, Elizabeth Gray: Rufus Jones and the Far East. Annual Quaker Lecture, October 19, 1958, High Point 1958.

– Vining, Elizabeth Gray: Rufus Jone's Mystik, in: Der Quäker. Monatsschrift der deutschen Freunde, 33, 1, 1959, 19-22.

– Moore, James Floyd: Rufus Jones. Luminous friend, Greensboro, ca. 1959 (Ninth Annual Ward Lecture 1958).

– Moore, James Floyd: The ethical thought of Rufus Matthew Jones. With special reference to biblical influences. Dissertation Boston 1960.

– Atkins, Gordon Charles: A critical examination of the mystical idealism of Rufus Matthew Jones. Dissertation University of Southern California 1960.

– Brinton, Howard: The revival movement in Iowa. A letter from Joel Bean to Rufus M. Jones, in: Bulletin of Friends' Historical Association, 50, 2, 1961, 102-110.

– Ammerman, Calvin Park: The moral philosophy of Rufus Jones. Dissertation The Iliff School of Theology 1963.

– Moore, J. Floyd: Rufus Jones. Quaker prophet. Reflections on the life and thought of the late mystic and philosopher whose centennial is being observed this week, in: Christian Century. An ecumenical weekly, 80, 4, 1963, 107-108.

– Vining, Elizabeth Gray: Rufus Jones, teacher, in: Friends Journal, 9, 2, 1963, 29-30.

– Vining, Elisabeth Gray: Rufus Jones, in: Der Quäker. Monatsschrift der deutschen Freunde, 37, 2, 1963, 190-192.

– Cain, Glen T.: The place of Christ in the theology of Rufus M. Jones. Dissertation Duke University 1963.

– Moore, James Floyd: The Rufus Jones Centennial, in: Friends World News. Bulletin of the Friends' World Committee for Consultation, 69, 1963, 3-5.

– Doncaster, Hugh: His Life (Rufus M. Jones, 1863-1948, 1), in: The Friend. The Quaker weekly journal, 121, 4, 1963, 92-94.

– Doncaster, Hugh: His significance to the Society of Friends. (Rufus M. Jones, 1863-1948, 2), in: The Friend. The Quaker weekly journal, 121, 5, 1963, 124-125.

– Steere, Douglas: Rufus Jones as teacher, in: The Friend. The Quaker weekly journal, 121, 6, 1963, 155-156.

– Hadley, Herbert: American observance of the Rufus Jones centenary, in: The Friend. The Quaker weekly journal, 121, 6, 1963, 154.

– Steere, Douglas: The scholarship of Rufus Jones, in: The Friend. The Quaker weekly journal, 121, 7, 1963, 188-189.

– Rufus Jones spricht (Eine Zusammenstellung im "Friends Journal" v. 15.01.63), in: Der Quäker. Monatsschrift der deutschen Freunde, 38, 1, 1964, 7-12.

– Ting, Simon: Rufus Jones and Lao Tzu, in: Ching Feng, 8, 3/4, 1964, 31-56.

– Caffrey, Augustine: The affirmation mysticism of Rufus Matthew Jones. Dissertation Catholic University 1967.

– Elliott, Errol T.: Quakers on the American frontier. A history of the westward migrations, settlements, and developments of Friends on the American continent, Richmond 1969.

– Watson (MacLaren) to Rufus Jones. 1850-1950, Waco 1971 (20 Centuries of Great Preaching, 7).

– Holdsworth, Christopher: Mystics and heretics in the Middle Ages. Rufus Jones reconsidered. Presidential address to the Friends' Historical Society, 1972, in: The Journal of the Friend's Historical Society, 53, 1, 1972, 9-30.

– Cadbury, Henry: Friendly heritage. Letters from the Quakers past, Norwalk 1972.

Newman, Daisy: A procession of Friends. Quakers in America, New York 1972 (Religion in America Series).

– Durnbaugh, Donald: Baptists and Quakers. Left wing Puritans?, in: Quaker History. The Bulletin of Friends' Historical Association, 62, 2, 1973, 67-82.

– Bassuk, Daniel Eliot: The secularisation of mysticism. An analysis and critique of the mystical in Rufus Jones and Martin Buber. Dissertation Drew University 1974.

– Bassuk, Daniel Eliot: Secularisation of mysticism. An analysis and critique of the mystical in Rufus Jones and Martin Buber, in: Drew Gateway, 46, 1-3, 1975/76, 106-107.

– Hinshaw, Seth B.: Quaker influence on American ideals. An overview, n.p., 1976. Reprint n.p., 1982.

– Jones, Rufus Matthew, in: Bowden, Henry Warner; Gaustad, Edwin (ed.): Dictionary of American religious biography, Westport 1977, 138-139.

– Tucher, Heinz von: Rufus Jones - Quäker Prophet!, in: Der Quäker. Monatsschrift der deutschen Freunde, 52, 5, 1978, 95-96.

– Leonard, Bill J.: American Mysticism. The inner authority, in: Review and Expositor, 75, 1978, 276-278.

– Newby, James R.: Reflections from the light of Christ. Five Quaker classics, Richmond 1980.

– Endy, Melvin B.: The interpretation of Quakerism. Rufus Jones and his critics, in: Quaker History. The Bulletin of Friends' Historical Association, 62, 1, 1981, 3-21.

– Wilson, Robert: Philadelphia Quakers 1681-1981, Philadelphia 1981.

– Moss, Jean Dietz: Godded with God. Hendrick Niclaes and his family of love, Philadelphia 1981 (Transactions of the American Philosophical Society, 71).

– Gwyn, Douglas Phillip: The apocalyptic word of God. The life and message of George Fox (1624-1691). Dissertation Drew University 1982.

– Kenworthy, Leonard S.: Luminous Friend, in: Kenworthy, Leonard S.: (ed.): In the U.S.A. Kennett Square, ca. 1984, 115-130 (Living in the Light, 1).

– Punshon, John: Portrait in grey. A short history of the Quakers, London 1984. London 1986². Reprint London 1991.

– Alten, Diana: Rufus Jones and the American Friend. A quest for unity, in: Quaker History. The Bulletin of Friends' Historical Association, 74, 1, 1985, 41-48.

– Bronner, Edwin B.: Jones, Rufus Matthew, in: Josephson, Harold (ed.): Biographical dictionary of modern peace leaders, London 1985, 474-475.

– Crosfield, John F.: A history of the Cadbury Family. 2 vol., London 1985.

– Jones, Mary Hoxie: Rufus Matthew Jones. Mystic, in: Mystics Quarterly, 12, 1, 1986, 14-18.

– Kohrman, Allan: Respectable pacifists. Quaker response to World War I., in: Quaker History. The Bulletin of Friends' Historical Association, 75, 1, 1986, 41-48.

– Kent, Stephen A.: Psychology and Quaker mysticism. The legacy of William James and Rufus Jones, in: Quaker History. The Bulletin of Friends' Historical Association, 76, 1, 1987, 1-17.

– Kent, Stephen: Psychological and mystical interpretations of early Quakerism. William James and Rufus Jones, in: Religion. A journal of religion and religions, 17, 1987, 251-274.

– Coward, Harold G.: A modern protestant mystic, in: Indian Philosophical Annual, 17, 1987, 84-95.

– Mongar, Jack: Are Quaker mystics?, in: The Friends' Quarterly, 25, 3, 1988, 117-125.

– Damiano, Kathryn: On earth as it is in heaven: Eighteenth century Quakerism as realized eschatology. Dissertation Cincinnati 1988.

– Phillips, Brian David: Friendly patriotism. British Quakerism and the imperial nation, 1890-1910, Dissertation Cambridge 1989.

– Cooper, Wilmer: Jones, Rufus Mattew, in: Reid, Daniel (ed.): Dictionary of Christianity in America, Downers Grove 1990, 601-602.

– Jones, Rufus Matthew, in: Bowden, John: Who's Who in Theology, London 1990, 67.

– Oliver, John: J. Walter Malone: The American Friend and an evangelical Quaker's social agenda, in: Quaker History. The Bulletin of Friends' Historical Association, 80, 2, 1991, 63-84.

– Rufus Matthew Jones, in: Roberts, Nancy, L.: American peace writers, editors, and periodicals, New York 1991, 147-148.

– Collett, Stephen: Quaker concerns in a world which seeks peace, in: Practiced in the presence, Richmond 1994, 179-188.

– Cooper, Wilmer: The legacy of Rufus M. Jones, in: Practiced in the Presence, Richmond 1994, 15-35.

– Barbour, Hugh: Liberal pastors and new intellectual meetings, 1900-1945, in: Barbour, Hugh (ed.): Quaker crosscurrents. Three hundred years of Friends in the New York Meetings, Syracuse 1995, 222-238.

– Heron, Alastair: Quakers in Britain. A century of change. 1895-1995, Kelso 1995.

– Barbour, Hugh: Rufus Jones and Quaker unity, in: Anderson, Paul; Macey, Howard (ed.): Truth's bright embrace, Newberg 1996, 117-131.

– Schmitt, Hans A.: Quakers and Nazis. Inner light in outer darkness, Columbia 1997.

– Barbour, Hugh: Jones, Rufus Matthew, in: ANB, XII, 1999, 238-239.

– Cazden, Elizabeth: Rufus Matthew Jones - Brief life of a practical mystic: 1863-1948, in: Harvard Magazine, 1999, 101, 5, 5-6.

– Angell, Stephen W.: Rufus Jones and the Laymen's Missions inquiry: How a Quaker helped to shape modern ecumenical Christianity, in: Quaker Theology. A progressive journal and forum for discussion and study, 2, 3, 2000, 167-209.

– Benson, Lewis: "Das von Gott in jedem Menschen". Was meinte George Fox damit? Dortmund 2001.

– Hall, David: The study of eighteenth-century English Quakerism. From Rufus Jones to Larry Ingle, in: Quaker Studies, 5, 2, 2001, 105-119.

– Kennedy, Thomas C.: British Quakerism. 1860-1920. The transformation of a religious community, New York 2001.

– Jarman, Roswitha: Vom Wesen und Werk der Liebe, Bad Pyrmont 2002 (Richard-L. Cary-Vorlesung, 2002).

– Cazden, Elizabeth: Jones, Rufus Matthew (1863-1948), in: Abbott, Margery Post; Chijioke, Mary Ellen; Dandelion, Pink; Oliver, John W. (ed.): Historical Dictionary of the Friends (Quakers), Lanham 2003, 145-146 (Religions, Philosophies, and Movements Series, 46).

– Hedstrom, Matthew S.: Rufus Jones and mysticism for the masses, in: Cross Currents, 54, 2, 2004, 31-44.

– Cooper, Wilmer A.: Reflections on Rufus M. Jones: Quaker giant of the twentieth century, in: Quaker History, XCIV, 2, 2005, 25-43.

– Blamires, David: Eckhart, Rufus Jones and the Quaker tradition, in: The Friends Quarterly, XXXV, 3, 2006, 100-109.

– Schwartz, Ed (ed.): Title faithful voices. Oral readings, exploring beliefs in action. Philadelphia 2006.

– Cortright, David: Gandhi and beyond. Nonviolence for an age of terrorism. Boulder 2006.

www.ingramcontent.com/pod-product-compliance
Lightning Source LLC
Chambersburg PA
CBHW070923150426
42812CB00049B/1371